THE ELEMENTS OF THE GREEK TRADITION

Murry Hope is one of the foremost authors on esoteric wisdom, ancient magical religions and related subjects. She was the co-founder of *The Atlanteans* society in 1957 and served as its president, principal teacher and healer for twenty of the forty years she has been engaged in metaphysical studies. She has worked as a journalist, teacher, lecturer and professional classical singer. In 1988 she established the *Institute for the Study and Development of Transpersonal Sensitivity* in the USA. Murry has published many books, run lectures and seminars, and appeared on radio and television worldwide in her capacity as an expert in this field.

THE ELEMENTS OF

THE GREEK TRADITION

Murry Hope

ELEMENT BOOKS

© Murry Hope 1989

First published in 1989 by
Element Books Limited
Longmead, Shaftesbury, Dorset

Printed and bound in Great Britain by Billings,
Hylton Road, Worcester

Designed by Jenny Liddle
Illustrations by Martin Jones
Cover design by Max Fairbrother
Cover illustration by Jeremy Norton

Typeset by Photoprint, Torquay, Devon

British Library Cataloguing in Publication Data
Hope, Murry
The elements of the Greek tradition.
1. Greek myths, ancient period. Psychological
I. Title
292'.13

ISBN 1–85230–112–0

CONTENTS

To Ian, my friend of many years whose archaeological work has contributed much to this book, with gratitude

INTRODUCTION

The classics have formed the basis of Western education for centuries. Their strange tales of gods, godlings, heroes and mythical beasts have captured the imagination of a succession of intellects from all spheres of life – scholarship, architecture, art, politics, education . . . and, yet, on the surface they would appear to contain nothing more than a set of irrational fables which, if taken out of their classical context, would be viewed as little more than fairy-tales by most thinking people.

Disguised within the tales of immortals, monsters, heroes and elements of nature consciousness that dominate Greek mythology, however, lies a deep and accurate assessment of the human psychological condition. This suggests that the originators of many of these parables, if not those who actually recorded them centuries later, were fully cognisant of the deeper functions of the human mind. What is more, they also provide us with guidelines for controlling the ever-expanding mental powers that are our natural heritage. Who these people were or where they came from is part of another enquiry, but this should not prevent the reader from arriving at his or her own conclusions, the field being open for investigation at all levels.

As is inevitably the case with advanced knowledge, the true nature of which, like a Chinese whisper, has become obscured by the diverse interpretations it has been given over the centuries, much of what was originally advanced scientific and psychological thinking has degenerated into suspect magical practices. Added to this mixture are those primitive rites that played such an important role in the lives of many early cultures. Together they make the myths, magic and mysticism of ancient Greece.

Unravelling these many threads is no new exercise, however. The sages and scholars of the classical era made a fairly good job of it, and we are indebted to them for the notion that there might conceivably be more behind Greek mythology than appears at first glance. The fact that it carries a subconscious message is to be evidenced in the interest and respect paid to it by so many great minds over the centuries.

Modern psychology has also been quick to acknowledge its deeper significance and, as Carl Jung so wisely commented:

> What we are to our inward vision, and what man appears to be *sub specie aternitatis*, can only be expressed by way of myth. Myth is more individual and expresses life more precisely than does science. Science works with concepts of averages which are far too general to do justice to the subjective variety of an individual life.[1]

[1] Jung, C. G., *Memories, Dreams and Reflections* (Fontana, 1983).

1·FORMATION AND EARLY HISTORY

In order to understand something of the nature of the myths and magic of ancient Greece, it is necessary to look at the historical and cultural backcloth against which they were etched. To effect an adequate summary of those times would, however, require more space than this book allows, so I trust the ensuing summary will suffice to convey the general picture.

In the basin of the Aegean Sea, a Mediterranean or Minoan civilisation existed that flourished in Crete, *circa* 3000–1400 BC. However, it was not until the sixteenth century BC, when it reached its apogee, that continental Greece initially savoured its influence, Mycenae (Argolis) being the first Greek city to absorb its cultural impact. It brought prosperity through trade and heralded the Classical Age. We are indebted to archaeology for much of the information available regarding pre-Mycenaean culture, which appeared to follow the pattern exhibited by most earlier societies. Fetishism – the worship of sacred stones and places – cults of pillars, weapons, trees, animals and other animistic trends prevailed and, in later times, when an anthropomorphic conception of divinity eventually came into being the Cretan pantheon was formed and the myths were born.

Many Greek legends contain elements of earlier Cretan myths and a short study will serve to highlight the occurrences of these superimpositions – the birth of Zeus in Crete, Europa and the Bull, the Cretans brought by Apollo to Delphi to be priests of his cult and

1

the story of the Minotaur being good examples. Once they had assumed their positions in continental Greece, however, the old Aegean divinities took on Hellenistic aspects and, in the course of time, their original physiognomy slowly disappeared.

The Cretan pantheon was essentially feminine, its principle deity being the Great Goddess or Universal Mother in whom were united all the functions and attributes of divinity. Representations of the Goddess varied with different epochs, the best-known portrayal probably being the Cretan version, which shows her in a flounced skirt with exposed breasts, wearing an elaborate turban or head-dress. She is also frequently depicted holding serpents or with the serpent motif emblazoned on her garments. It is questionable, however, whether a single divinity was involved. What is more likely is that each town, city or province had its own version of the Goddess, which was naturally flavoured by the activities, trades or talents dominant among its people. Names that appear in this context include Rhea, Dictynna and Britomartis, although the latter, which translates as 'the sweet virgin', would appear to have little in common with the maternal aspect of the Goddess.

The Cretans also acknowledged a subordinate god who bore the epithet *asterius* – the starry – a name that surfaces later in the form of Asterios, king of Crete, who married Europa, following her adventure with Zeus. He was eventually assimilated into Zeus himself, whose legend was enriched by its Cretan contribution.

The old Cretan god's one distinction was the mingling of animal and human features that made up his nature. The Minotaur is analogous to the bull god of the Elamites and to Enki of the Sumerians. In fact, the cult of the bull, which was so prevalent in those times, is believed by many astrologers to be related to the Solar Age of Taurus, through which our planet was then believed to have been passing.

How, then – and when – did the Greek pantheon first come into existence and what were the forces that influenced its eventual manifestation? The two main works from which we elicit our information, *The Iliad* and *The Odyssey*, are attributed to Homer and clearly derive from orally transmitted traditions describing the events of the Trojan war (*circa* 1200 BC) and its aftermath. The epics mix fact with fantasy and embody the myths of ancient Greece.

According to Homer, Oceanus (or Okeanos) and his spouse Tethys spawned both gods and mortals. Oceanus was traditionally a river god, but his river was no ordinary one. It represented the veil or boundary between this world and the next and, 'Ever since the time when everything originated from him he has continued to flow to the outermost edge of the earth, flowing backwards upon himself in a circle'.[1] That these myths have a cosmic content may be evidenced by the fact that, in this particular myth, Oceanus and Tethys refrain from breeding for some time, as they frequently quarrelled. In other words, the myth is telling us that in our planet's early days, life as we know it did not exist and only came into being when Earth had assumed some form of stability that rendered it suitable for use by various other forms of life.

Later in their history the Greeks thought it proper to provide their gods with a genealogy and a history. Hesiod's *Theogony*, written *circa* eighth century BC, is the oldest Greek attempt at mythological classification. It presented a cosmogony, as much as a theogony, that was officially recognised as worthy of some status or general acceptance within the communities of the time. Although the more familiar Greek divinities make their appearance in the *Iliad* and *Odyssey*, the poet tells us nothing of their origins. The sea theme appears to predominate, however, in keeping with early Egyptian depictions of the birthplace of the gods as being some watery Eden to the west.

From the sixth century BC onwards, however, until the commencement of the Christian era, other theogonies, which departed widely from the Hesiodic traditions, emerged under the influence of Orphism. The Orphic mysteries were not normally available to the general public of the time as they carried too strong an Asiatic flavour to be specifically Greek in character. Tracing the genealogy of the Greek pantheons, therefore, necessitates an examination of the main Greek Creation myths, these being:

- the Homeric Creation Myth
- the Pelasgian Creation Myth
- the Orphic Creation Myth and
- the Olympian Creation Myth.

THE HOMERIC CREATION MYTH

Graves sees Homer's version of the creation myth as synonymous with that of the Pelasgians, since Tethys reigned over the sea like Eurynome, and Oceanus girdled the Universe, as did Ophion, which suggests that the poet was obviously influenced from this quarter.

THE PELASGIAN CREATION MYTH

In the beginning, Eurynome, the Goddess of all things, rose naked from Chaos, but finding nothing substantial upon which to rest her feet, she divided the sea from the sky, set the winds in motion and commenced the work of creation. The great serpent Ophion was her first effort and, after coupling with him she assumed the form of a dove and laid the universal egg. At her bidding Ophion coiled seven times around this egg until it finally hatched, splitting in two. Out tumbled all that exists: Eurynome's children, the Sun, Moon, planets, stars and the Earth as we see and know them. Eurynome and Ophion made their home on Mount Olympus, but he upset her by claiming that the universe was *his* creation, so she bruised his head with her heel, kicked out his teeth and banished him to the dark caves below the earth. Shades of later Christian depictions of the Virgin Mary crushing the head of Lucifer in serpent form!

In the Egyptian myth, Ra assumes the Eurynome role with his old enemy, Typhon, as the proud serpent who is put to flight by Ra's daughter, Bast, the Cat Goddess. A supreme example of a single-source legend, the archetypal significance of which is obviously coloured by currently fashionable trends in religious and philosophical thought.

Eurynome next created the seven planetary powers, setting a Titaness and Titan over each: Theia and Hyperion for the Sun, Phoebe and Atlas for the Moon, Dione and Crius for Mars, Metis and Coeus for Mercury, Themis and Eurymedon for Jupiter, Tethys and Oceanus for Venus, Rhea and Cronus for Saturn. The first man, however, was Pelasgus, ancestor of the Pelasgians, who, '. . . sprang from the soil of Arcadia, followed by certain others, whom he taught to make huts, feed upon acorns, and sew pigskin tunics such as poor folk still wear in Euboea and Phocis'.[2] It appears, therefore, that, at some point in their distant past, the Pelasgians came into contact with a sophisticated theogony that influenced both their culture and lifestyle.

THE ORPHIC CREATION MYTH

According to Orphic tradition, black-winged night, a goddess who even the major gods held in awe, was courted by the Wind and laid a silver egg in the womb of Darkness. From this egg Eros emerged to set the universe in motion. Eros was double-sexed, golden winged, had four heads and sometimes roared like a bull, hissed like a serpent or bleated like a ram. Night named him both Ericepaius and Protegenus Phaeton and dwelt with him in a cave. She displayed herself as a triad: Might, Order and Justice. Before this cave sat the Mother Goddess, Rhea, playing on a brass drum to compel man to attend to her oracles. Eros (also called Phanes) created Earth, Sky, Sun and

Moon, but the triple goddess ruled the universe and her sceptre passed to Uranus.

The cosmic egg theme constantly recurs in early myths and has possible connections with the original seeding of this planet that, according to certain secret arcane traditions, was generated from the binary star Sirius and concerned a race of people from this star who reproduced themselves through an external ova system, the fertilised seed growing in egg form *outside* the womb and not by means of an extended period of internal gestation, as is the case in human beings.

Another point worth mentioning regarding this particular creation myth is the description accorded to Eros. Eros is dually sexed (has the anima and animus in balance), has four heads (has realised the four-fold nature of a spiritually ascended being – the elemental qualities having been negotiated and mastered), and is therefore representative of the love principle in its higher, purer octaves. The triple goddess story obviously relates to the pre-Aryan goddess cults that predominated in the Silver Age, whose influence is still to be found in Wicca and among those who have striven to re-establish the older pre-Christian faiths in a profound effort to discover their real spiritual roots.

Three distinct influences emerge from this enquiry: the obvious and well-documented matriarchal tradition, the more violent patriarchal deities or conquerors who assumed control by force and the deeper, more significant strain that echoed profoundly throughout the pantheons of those early periods, alerting the sensitive to its pre-Flood or intercosmic message.

THE OLYMPIAN CREATION MYTH

According to Hesiod, in the beginning was Chaos, vast and dark. Then appeared Gaia, the deep-breasted Earth and finally Eros, the 'love that softens hearts'. From Chaos were born Erebus and Night who, in uniting, gave birth to Ether and Hemera. Gaia bore Uranus, the sky crowned with stars 'whom she made her equal in grandeur so that he entirely covered her'.[3] Then she created the high mountains and the sterile sea with its harmonious waves. Prior to the establishment of the Olympian dynasty Gaia reigned supreme. Not only did she create the universe and bear the race of gods, but she also created man. Is it not interesting to observe how the majority of the early creation myths feature a creatrix rather than a creator? Gaia was also a goddess of prophecy, the oracle at Delphi having originally belonged to her before it passed into Apollo's hands at a later date.

She was venerated at Dodona, Tegea, Sparta and at Athens near Areopagus.

The universe having been formed, all that remained was for the gods to people it. Gaia (Earth), united with her son Uranus (Heaven), to produce the first race, the Titans, a name that derives from the Cretan word for 'King'. Here we have another of those 'sons of god and daughters of men' themes with which we are constantly being confronted in the myths of many early cultures.

In Greece, the Titans were ultimately honoured as the ancestors of men and to them was attributed the invention of the arts and magic. This suggests some external influence, probably from Atlantis, the Atlanteans (according to arcane tradition) sharing one thing in common with the Titans – stature, as both were believed to have been above average height. This would also account for the Promethean myth, Prometheus being the Titan who incurred the wrath of Zeus by favouring mankind with the gift of fire. The early Greek legends certainly lend credence to similar stories of an advanced people who appeared as from nowhere, bringing with them civilisation and some form of technology.

There were, we are told, 12 Titans (a number that is highly significant in Greek Magic and mysticism) – six males and six females. They were named Oceanus, Coeus, Hyperion, Crius, Iapetus, Cronus, Theia, Rhea, Mnemosyne, Phoebe, Tethys and Themis. Uranus and Gaia then produced the Cyclopes, Brontes, Steropes and Arges, who resembled the other gods but had only one eye in the middle of their forehead. Finally, they bore three monsters – Cottus, Briareus and Gyges, called the Hecatoncheires or Centimanes, whose horrific appearance so disturbed their father that, as soon as they were born, he shut them up in the depths of the earth.

Gaia, it seemed, rather resented this rejection of her offspring and planned a terrible revenge on her spouse. From gleaming steel she fashioned a sickle or *harpe*, but when she told her children of her plan they were horrified and refused to cooperate. Only Cronus, her last born, agreed to carry out the dastardly deed. Night came and Uranus joined his wife, unsuspectingly falling asleep. Cronus, who had been hidden in the bedchamber by his mother, castrated his father with the sickle, throwing his testicles into the sea. From the terrible wound, black blood dropped, fertilising Earth which consequently gave birth to the Furies – another set of monstrous giants – and to the ash tree nymphs – the Meliae. The debris that floated on the surface of the waves became a white foam, from which the beautiful love goddess, Aphrodite, was born.

The cosmological nature of this myth accords with the legends of

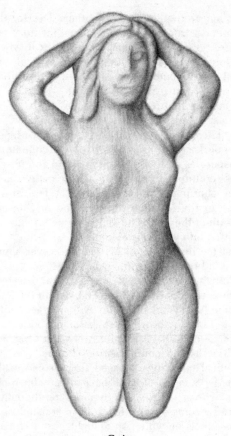

Gaia

other earlier nations, notably those of Sumeria, Mesopotamia, Asia and South America. The *Popul Vuh* (the Holy Book of the Incas) tells us that 'the sea boiled up and sticky substances rained from the sky', while similar floods and disasters are also recorded in the Babylonian Gilgamesh epic, Hebrew legends and secret Egyptian traditions that have been handed down via occult sources through the centuries. The Chinese believed these events to have taken place in the reign of the Emperor Yaltou, during which time there was no light for four days and after which a great star with a tail appeared in the sky.

Personally, I do not see all these myths as relating to the same catastrophes. Some are more concerned with the lead up to and events subsequent to the Flood, while others describe the arrival of comets or similar astronomical phenomena, memory being a great bender of time. Sorting the magical and mystical wheat from the chaff of folklore, tribal superstition and historical vagaries is a Herculean task and a combination of logic and intuition is the best ally in the quest for transcendental truth.

The Titan Iapetus had four sons: Menoetius, Atlas, Prometheus and Epimetheus. Menoetius and Atlas were punished for their part in the Titans' later revolt against the Olympians, Menoetius being despatched to darkest Erebus while Atlas was condemned to stand before the Hesperides on the edge of the world and bear the vault of heaven on his shoulders. Prometheus, whose main weapon appears to have been cunning, enjoyed a different fate and played an important role in the legendary history and origins of humanity. During the revolt of the Titans he kept a prudent neutrality and was actually admitted into the circle of immortals. He entertained a silent grudge against the destroyers of his race, however, and constantly favoured mankind rather than the gods.

Legend tells us that Prometheus, using clay and water (according to some, his own tears) fashioned the first men in the likeness of the gods, into whom Athene breathed life. A similar account also occurs in the Adam and Eve myth, which suggests that both stories derived from the same source. The Talmudic Archangel Michael is seen by some authorities as the counterpart of Prometheus, while those enigmatic Biblical couplings engaged in by some exalted race of beings and the womenfolk of Earth have already been observed.

Prometheus, whose name is said to mean 'forethought' and 'swastika', was said by some authorities to have assisted in the birth of Athene, in payment for which she taught him architecture, astronomy, mathematics, navigation, medicine, metallurgy and other useful arts, which he duly passed on to the beings he created. He is also reputed to have given mankind the gift of fire, which, according to one story, he stole from the forge of Hephaestus. Another myth, however, informs us that he lit a torch from the sun's fiery chariot. From the torch he broke a glowing fragment of charcoal, which he thrust into the hollow of a giant fennel stalk. After extinguishing the torch, he stole away undiscovered to pass on the narthex containing his gift to the race he had created. Either way, Zeus was outraged by the theft and ordered Hephaestus to fashion clay and water into a body of great beauty that would equal an immortal goddess, at least in appearance! All the divinities bestowed gifts upon this artificial creature, who was called Pandora, except Hermes whose offering consisted of a warped mind. Zeus then sent her as a gift to Prometheus' brother Epimetheus and, although the former warned his sibling against accepting gifts from Olympus, Epimetheus was so dazzled by her beauty that he welcomed her and made a place for her among men. Now Pandora carried in her arms a great vase, incorrectly described as a box. When she raised the lid its contents, all but one of which were terrible afflictions, escaped and spread across the earth. Only the kindly Hope did not fly away.

There are conflicting stories concerning the outcome of the Pandora-Epimetheus episode. One we have just mentioned, but, according to another, Epimetheus was tricked into marrying the foolish, mischievous and idle android, and allowed her to open the jar in spite of his brother's warning. I cannot help wondering whether those prophetic sages of the past were not warning us against the folly of being taken in at some future date by the beauty and questionable efficiency of gadgetry!

Another interesting point, which is later borne out in alchemy, is Hermes' dubious gift to Pandora. Carl Jung sees the Mercurius as representative of the element of chaos, which is essential to growth in that the emergence from chaos to order, via the application of will and the process of transcendental realisation, is a crucial factor in the development of all thinking beings.

Zeus, it seems, was still not pacified so he resolved to annihilate the human race with a deluge. Once again Prometheus gave his aid to mankind by warning his son, Ducalion who, on the advice of his father, constructed an ark in which to take refuge when the waters rose. For nine days and nine nights Ducalion and his wife floated on the risen tides, but on the tenth day the downpour ceased and the two survivors were able to disembark on the crest of Mount Othrys or Mount Parnassus. Ducalion made haste to offer a sacrifice to Zeus and the god, touched by his piety, promised to grant him his first wish. Ducalion requested the renewal of the human race.

Although Prometheus' cunning helped to keep him in circulation for a long time, Zeus' ire eventually got the better of him and the Father of the Gods had the unfortunate Titan chained naked to a pillar in the Caucasian mountains where a greedy vulture tore at his liver all day, year in and year out. There was no end to his torment because every night the liver regrew. Prometheus was eventually released by the kindness of Chiron during the course of Hercules' fourth Labour.

According to the Egyptians, Prometheus was a son of Poseidon, which is another way of saying that he represented a person or persons who hailed from across the seas. In view of the gifts he supposedly bestowed upon the then uncivilised world, he is probably representative of a race or culture rather than a singular being, but then I am not alone in associating one branch of the Titans at least with the peoples of the Old Country (Atlantis).

The metaphysical inferences in the Prometheus story are obvious. There is the ever-recurring theme of a race of people who possessed advanced technological and metaphysical knowledge that they saw fit to bestow upon people who were neither spiritually nor physically advanced enough to handle it. Prometheus, therefore, belongs among those wisdom deities who suffered for the redemption of mankind, but also gained knowledge and furthered their own spiritual evolution in the process.

Our final myth for consideration in this chapter concerns the mythological ages of man. Kerenyi tells us that there were originally four distinct ages or races, but Hesiod described five of them, '. . . since he did not wish to identify our heroes either with the race of bronze or with his own race, that of iron. He attributed the origin even of the first race – that of gold – to the Olympian gods, which was not entirely correct, as he himself states that at this time Kronos still ruled, and not the later Olympians'.[4]

THE GOLDEN AGE

The first men of this race lived like gods while Cronus reigned. Free from worry and fatigue, old age did not afflict them and they rejoiced in continual festivity. Hesiod emphasises that they were not immortal, but died peacefully as in 'sweet slumber'. All the blessings of the world were theirs – the fruitful earth gave forth its unbidden treasures and the people ate honey and drank the milk of goats. After their death they became benevolent genii, protectors and tutelary guardians of the living. They bestowed good fortune, were patrons of music and helped men to uphold justice if their spiritual advice was heard and heeded. Shades of the Irish Tuatha de Danaans.

THE SILVER AGE

The ensuing race was believed by the sages to have been much inferior, resembling the golden race neither in body nor soul. It equates with the dominance of matrism and has strong lunar connotations. The people of those times were mainly agriculturalists who did not indulge in war, were vegetarians and lived to a ripe old age. Their menfolk, however, were subject to their mothers, which naturally failed to meet with the approval of Hesiod who described them as disputatious and lacking in manliness. Neither did they offer sacrifice to Zeus, which angered the god to the extent that he eventually destroyed them, after which they sank into the depths of the earth to appear in later myth as the subterranean blessed, in which capacity they were accorded some small, if insignificant, degree of veneration. The Silver Age is sometimes designated as the Minoan period, although most authorities equate it with the times just prior to and directly after the Flood, when goddess worship predominated throughout Europe and the Middle East.

THE BRAZEN OR BRONZE AGE

The people of this age were entirely different from their silver predecessors: they 'fell like the fruit from ash trees', were robust and delighted only in oaths, meat-eating and war-like exploits, 'Their pitiless hearts were hard as steel, their might was untameable, their arms invincible'.[5] According to one source they ended by cutting each others throats, while another account has it that 'black death' seized upon them all. These were doubtless our invaders from the north who worked in bronze, the ash tree (Yggdrasil) holding great significance in their religious beliefs.

THE IRON AGE

Hesiod gives us some variations on this theme, declaring that, prior to the Iron Age, Zeus created a race of divine heroes – those who fought the famous wars for Thebes or Troy. They were more righteous and better than the Bronze Age people and, after death, they came to the Isles of the Blessed, which were girdled by Oceanus. In these idyllic islands the life-giving fields bear sweet fruit thrice yearly and Cronus, set free of his chains by Zeus, rules in peace and harmony.

For the Iron Age, however, Hesiod had nothing but abuse, being obsessed with gloomy prophesies about the birth of grey-haired children and the return of the goddesses Aidos and Nemesis to Olympus, leaving mankind to perish undefended. The Iron Age is generally associated with misery, crime, treachery and cruelty, when, 'men respect neither vows, justice, nor virtue'. This explanation is said to account for what is seen as the progressive degeneracy of man and, as must now be obvious to the reader, represents the age in which we live at present.

It is comforting to observe that Hesiod dreamed of a golden age, or, Utopia where peace, harmony and justice reigned, just as many of us do today. No doubt, we who yearn for that glorious past, are fragments of the same group-soul as the Greek poet, the memory of another place and another way of living being programmed into both our genes and our collective unconscious. We can but live in the pious hope that at some point in the future the ouroboric circle will be completed and a new Golden Age of enlightenment will reunite our race in happiness, understanding and love. Cronus will once again rule, or in other words, Time heals all.

[1] *Kerenyi, C., The Gods of the Greeks (Thames & Hudson, 1979).*
[2] *Graves, R., The Greek Myths (Penguin, 1984).*
[3] *Larousse Encyclopedia of Mythology (Hamlyn, 1959).*
[4] *Kerenyi, C., The Gods of the Greeks.*
[5] *Larousse Encyclopedia of Mythology.*

2·THE MOULDING

OF THE

GREEK ARCHETYPES

A question that is frequently asked is why, in view of the sublime nature of classical philosophy that, after all, constituted the state religion of classical Greece, were the deities of the Olympian pantheon assigned so many totally unspiritual and obviously human characteristics, many of which represented the less desirable traits of our race? In order to understand the psychology behind this it is necessary for us to join the myths just prior to the point at which the Olympians, under Zeus, effected their official take-over. The reasons for looking to this and other earlier sources will, I trust, soon become clear.

CRONUS, RHEA AND THE STONE

After Cronus had reduced his father, Uranus, to impotence, he liberated his brothers, the Titans (with the exception of the Cyclopes and Hecatoncheires) and set himself up as chief of the new dynasty. Creation continued with many more deities, mortals and fabulous beasts assuming identities and roles in the general picture. These are too numerous to merit description here, and no doubt constitute a mixture of religious allegory, nature entities and rulers who came and went. We can pick up the threads of the story, however, at the point where Cronus mated with his sister Rhea, who gave him three daughters – Hestia, Demeter and Hera – and three sons – Hades, Poseidon and Zeus.

An oracular prediction that one day Cronus would be overthrown by one of his children caused him great concern, so much so that he felt obliged to swallow each of them as they were born. Rhea was not unnaturally overwhelmed with grief and questioned why it should be her destiny to part with her offspring in this peculiar fashion. When the time approached for her to give birth to Zeus she sought the help of her own parents, Uranus and Gaia, to save the child. On their advice she travelled to Crete and brought forth her son in a deep cavern in the forests of Mount Aegeum. Gaia looked after the child while Rhea wrapped a large stone in swaddling clothes and presented it to Cronus who lost no time in swallowing it.

Gaia carried her grandson to Mount Ida (or Mount Dicte) where he was cared for by the nymphs Ida and Adrasteria, while the Curetes entertained the infant godling. According to some authorities the latter were a primitive tribe of the region, but the general opinion is that they were earth spirits or nature energies. Later they were deified for their service to the Father of the Gods and temples were erected to them, notably at Messina.

Safe from his father's ire, Zeus grew to manhood in the forests of Ida. His wet-nurse was Goat Amaltheia, a wondrous beast of whom even immortals were in awe. In gratitude Zeus placed her among the constellations and from her hide, which no arrow could pierce, the aegis was fashioned. To the nymphs he gave one of her horns, which contained an inexhaustible supply of whatever food or drink was desired. This became the famous cornucopia, or, horn of plenty – a symbol that also appears in the myths and legends of many other pantheons.

The oracle had not lied, however, and, upon attaining his majority, Zeus swore to punish his father. According to Apollodorus, the god summoned Metis (wisdom) to his aid and she administered to Cronus a drink that made him vomit up the stone, plus the children he had previously swallowed. Another version, however, insists that the special concoction was supplied by Rhea to Zeus, who laced his father's nectar, causing the same thing to happen.

Vanquished by his son's might, the old god was driven from the sky and despatched to some far-flung corner of the universe. So Homer has it, but other sources insist that he was sent to the ends of the Earth to dwell in bliss or plunged into mysterious slumber in Thule. Zeus placed the stone Cronus had disgorged at the foot of Mount Parnassus to bear witness to his victory and later it was displayed at Delphi for many years. The Olympian era had begun.

The disgorging of Rhea's five previous children would appear to correspond to an earlier Egyptian legend in which five intercalary days were added to the ancient calendar of 360 days, believed by some earlier cultures to have been the original measurement of one year. In the Egyptian myth these five extra days were gained through a game of draughts that the Egyptian Time Lord, Thoth, played with the Moon, from which he won 1/72nd part of her light – 1/72nd of 360 being exactly 5. Just as Zeus released his brothers, Hades and Poseidon, and his sisters, Hera, Hestia and Demeter, so Thoth was able to bring about the births of Isis, Osiris, Nephthys, Set and Horus.

All this suggests to me that both of these legends refer to an actual cosmological event that not only altered the orbit of the earth around the sun, and therefore the length of the calendar year, but also precipitated the end of a race or civilisation – the Titans of Greek mythology, Biblical pre-Flood peoples and Plato's Atlanteans.

In the story of the mutilation of Uranus, the message must surely be that an epoch in the Earth's evolutionary cycle was brought to an end by the passage of time, after which a gentle and more enlightened age (the Golden Age) emerged. Moving on once again, the oracular prediction regarding the eventual overthrow of Cronus would appear to suggest that certain far-seeing people, anticipating the onset of a new order, strove to suppress the oncoming tide of development, much of which appeared to them to be negative and retrogressive. The stone represented encapsulated energy which, when released, initiated the new age.

When viewed metaphysically, time is an energy in its own right that the people of the Golden Age were able to understand and manipulate, Cronus (time) being frequently depicted as the sickle-armed Grim Reaper. With the departure of the old god his energies were withdrawn, the implication being that this knowledge was lost.

THE WARS WITH THE TITANS AND GIANTS

Let us return once more to our myth. Zeus' newly released siblings made haste to persuade him to lead them in war against the Titans whose chieftain was Atlas. The Titans, with the exception of Oceanus, were jealous of the Olympians and wished to regain their status by reconquering the kingdom of which they had been dispossessed. After ten years of fighting, as had been prophesied, Zeus and his allies were the victors. The defeated Titans were bound in chains and cast into the depths of the Earth. Here we see the final downfall or end of those beings who were the teachers and allies of mankind, whoever they might have been. The records suggest a cosmological drama involving natural phenomena that preceded the better known Deluge.

The struggle with the Titans was followed by a war with the giants. These monstrous beings who had sprung from the blood of the mutilated Uranus were not only distinguished by their size, but also had, 'legs like serpents and their feet were formed of reptiles heads'. However, the gods alone were unable to triumph over these monstrosities – the help of a mortal was needed. This man was Hercules, whose nature and deeds we will be considering in a later chapter.

His new supremacy having been firmly established, Zeus – seen now as The Father of the Gods – set up his own immortal society, complete with laws and hierarchy. First came the 12 great gods and goddesses: Zeus himself, Poseidon, Hephaestus, Hermes, Ares and Apollo, Hera, Artemis, Hestia, Athene, Aphrodite and Demeter. Other divinities and godlings also shared the Olympic heights: Helios, Selene, Leto, Dione, Dionysus, Themis and Eros. The courtiers of the Olympians, sworn in their service, included the Horae, the Moerae, Nemesis, the Graces, the Muses, Iris, Hebe and Ganymede.

Hades, although the brother of Zeus, did not choose to reside on Olympus under his sibling's command, but preferred to dwell with his ladies – Persephone and Hecate – in his own subterranean empire. An arrangement had been effected between Zeus and his brothers that each should have his own territory. Zeus therefore ruled the sky, Poseidon the waters and Hades the Underworld. Although territorial disputes involving heroes, mortals and immortals did tend to arise from time to time, for the most part each brother kept his side of the bargain. There was, we are told, only one power to whom the Father of the Gods was subject – that of Moros, or destiny, although Aphrodite's famous Girdle was also a protection against his thunderbolts, and if she chose to deflect his shafts with its magical aid even Zeus could not win. A valid pointer towards the Love Ray in its purest form.

HOW THE DEITIES OF THE OLYMPIAN PANTHEON ACQUIRED HUMAN CHARACTERISTICS

The Olympians were credited with human passions and qualities. Love, hatred, anger and envy were known to them and they cruelly punished anyone who questioned their authority or stepped on their divine toes, but they could also shower favours upon those who revered and honoured them with gifts – a clear indication of a culture that imposed terrestrial values upon their Paradise and its resident deities. In other words, the people saw the gods in their own image and likeness, just as in our present day and age there are still many people who visualise God in some patriarchal form that accords with the customs and culture in which they have been raised.

Commenting on this fact, Carl Kerenyi refers to the many love escapades of Apollo, the greater number of which ended tragically, whether the object of the god's affection was male or female. Kerenyi writes:

> The reason why boys were numbered among the god's reputed lovers was that he himself was the god of just that age at which boys used to leave their mother's tutelage and live together. Their younger year-groups were subordinate to the older ones. They also attached themselves to individual older men. For boys as well as for girls this was the age of fugitive bloom. The tales represent Apollo's love, for a person of either sex, as having been very dangerous.[1]

From a metaphysical standpoint, the human characteristics bestowed on the Greek pantheon could be seen in the context of the Mirror Complex – the gods mirroring their invocators (or evocators as the case may be), like attracting like. People have, throughout time, fashioned their gods after their own image and likeness or according to their own needs. The prevailing climate of opinion among both rulers and ordinary folk demanded divinities to whose attributes they could understand and relate. It could be argued that the Egyptian deities did not conform to the same human standards as their Greek equivalents, but then the ancient Egyptians were a different race with their own special characteristics. Although Isis, Osiris and their family may have assumed kinder roles in relation to the human scheme of things, there was always their opponent, or, anti-ray to contend with in the form of Set.

In fact, the Olympians clearly reflect the psychology of both the Greeks of those times and the peoples of the surrounding cultures that were eventually absorbed into the Hellenistic ethos, if we are to believe the history books. For example, there was a broad division between the philosopher, warrior and merchant classes and the ordinary people who tilled the land and attended to the everyday affairs which constitute an important part of the economy of any nation. Philosophical thought and teaching, being both profound and enlightened, deemed it necessary to project these qualities onto an appropriate deity. The Warrior caste, however, also needed to be considered as the ordinary person relied upon it for protection of home and property. Athene, Goddess of Wisdom, was therefore also allotted the role of protectress and, given the way of war in those times, it became necessary for her to 'exceed even Ares' in fighting prowess and strategy.

However, the merchants, ever aware of the fact that both peace and war constituted possible avenues of revenue, saw no harm in assigning their particular brand of skills to the crafty Hermes, who could happily play one side against another should the necessity arise. Everyone likes to love and be loved and if that love, be it carnal or ethereal, can be kept well away from the battlefield, shop or senate, then so much the better. After all, who wants a love goddess who spends her time weaving when she could be accommodating some suitor! The beautiful Aphrodite was therefore forbidden to attend to anything other than amour! All in all we are presented with a nice set of social conveniences, neatly packaged in divine form.

Am I then inferring that there were no real gods or guiding 'Beings of Light' in the days of ancient Greece or in the ensuing classical period? By no means. Not every person living in those times saw Zeus as an oversexed monarch, Aphrodite as a divine prostitute or Hermes as a trickster. Each of these deities also had their positive aspects and, like attracting like, the pious devotee could just as likely contact a just Zeus, helpful Hermes or deeply caring Aphrodite. After all, these are but names that have been allotted to principles or impersonal energies, the manifestations of which are coloured by intention only. Nor did the Greeks see all their divinities in derogatory human terms – Hestia, for example, was nothing if not benign.

Philosophical enquiries of this nature were as prevalent in those far gone days as they are today. Epicurus (342?–270 BC), was founder and head of the philosophical school that bears his name. He was born on the island of Samos and taught at Athens from 306 BC onwards. On the subject of the gods he had this to say in a letter to Menoeceus.

First of all, believe that God is a being incorruptible (i.e., immortal and unchangeable) and blessed, just as in the common idea of God which is engraved on the mind, and do not assign to him anything contrary to his incorruption or unsuited to his blessedness, and believe about him whatever safeguards his blessedness and incorruption. For gods there certainly are, since the knowledge of them is a matter of immediate perception. But they are not what the majority of men believe them to be, in fact, they do not take care to represent them as they really believe them to be. And the irreligious man is not the one who denies the gods of the majority, but the one who applies to the gods the opinions of the majority. For what the majority say about the gods are not conceptions derived from sensation (*prolepseis*), but false suppositions (*hypolepseis*), according to which the greatest injuries overtake the wicked and the greatest blessings come to [the good] from the gods. For since men are always accustomed to their own virtues, they welcome those who are like themselves, but whatever is not of this sort they regard as alien.[2]

In the next chapter I hope to demonstrate how the sages and builders of the myths endeavoured to highlight the many ways in which we can experience the human condition, taking into account the numerous twists and turns in the psychology of humankind. In other words, it is not so much a question of the gods absorbing our characteristics as their showing us both what we are and what we should be.

[1] Kerenyi, C., *The Gods of the Greeks* (Thames & Hudson, 1979).
[2] Eliade, M., *From Primitives to Zen* (Collins, 1967).

3·THE TWELVE OLYMPIANS

Let us now take a look at the 12 main Olympian deities, their functions, respective archetypes and what they can tell us about ourselves.

ZEUS

ARCHETYPE

Patriarchal father, ruler/king.

PSYCHOLOGICAL EMPHASIS

The animus extravertedly expressed through the patriarchal mode.

THE MYTH

According to the *Larousse Encyclopedia of Mythology* (Hamlyn, 1959), the name 'Zeus' contains the Sanskrit root '*dyaus*' and the Latin '*dies*', which evoke the idea of the luminous sky. Zeus, therefore, ruled over the sky and all atmospheric phenomena — winds, clouds, rain and the destructive thunder and lightning came under his command. Being ruler of the sky he was venerated in lofty places, such as mountain tops. He had his own oracle at Dodona but occasionally borrowed Delphi from Apollo. The oak was sacred to him, as was the thunderbolt and the eagle and he is often depicted wearing a crown of oak leaves.

Zeus is shown as a man in the fullness of maturity, of robust body, with thick, dark, wavy or curly hair and a matching beard. He wears a long mantle that leaves his chest and right arm free. The sceptre of power is held in his left hand and the thunderbolt and eagle are at his feet. His magical colour is imperial purple.

Prior to installing Hera as first lady of Olympus, Zeus had several earlier unions, the first of which was with Metis (wisdom) whom, Hesiod informs us, 'knew more things than all the gods and men together'. Gaia and Uranus warned Zeus that, were he to have children with Metis they would be more powerful than he and would eventually dethrone him. So, when Metis was about to give birth to Athene, in order to forestall this happening Zeus swallowed the mother and her unborn child, thus avoiding any future problems and embodying wisdom.

His next love was Themis, daughter of Uranus and Gaia. Themis represented the Law that regulates both physical and moral order. Her children were the Horae (the hours or seasons), Eunomia (wise legislation), Dike (justice), Eirene (peace) and the Fates, or, Moerae, sometimes referred to as daughters of Night. Even though Zeus finally tied the matrimonial knot with Hera, Themis continued to remain near him as his adviser, which accounts for her presence in Olympia.

Although there are many legends concerning the divine courtship of Zeus and Hera, Pausanias' account is probably the best known. In this he describes how Zeus visited her in the form of a cuckoo in distress, upon which the kindly Hera took pity. Renowned for getting his own amorous way, Zeus promptly changed back into his Olympian form to claim the fulfilment of his desires, the Greek gods being adept at shape-shifting. Hera, however, resisted and it was not until he promised to marry her that she finally succumbed to his advances. The wedding was solemnly celebrated on Olympus, but it by no means put an end to Zeus' romantic inclinations, and Hera's jealousy and constant efforts to thwart her husband's affairs are well recorded in the classics.

HERA

ARCHETYPE

Queenly, aristocratic lady. Faithful, though jealous wife.

21

The anima introvertedly expressed through the possessive feminine mode.

THE MYTH

The name 'Hera' was originally believed to derive from the Latin 'herus' (master) and an old Greek word meaning 'earth', but now it is believed to be connected with the Sanskrit word 'svar' (the sky). So, like her celestial spouse, Hera was a deity of the upper regions of the air. Her esoteric attributes soon being forgotten or conveniently discarded by a people who were nothing if not terrestrial, she was designated patroness of marriage and all phases of feminine life.

Hera represents womanly stability in a male-orientated society, her only line of defence being her marital status. The cuckoo story is typical of the many ladies down the ages who have trapped their men into marriage by subterfuge. Hera is the faithful wife and mother forever hovering in the background, but, nevertheless, angered at her husband's infidelities, about which she appears to be able to do little in spite of her divine powers.

The Mother of the Gods is usually depicted as a woman of severe beauty and nobility. She wears a veil and is clothed as would befit the modesty of a matron of the classical period. Her daughter Hebe is often shown beside her mother. Her symbols are the peacock, a sceptre surmounted by a cuckoo and a pomegranate (representing conjugal love and fruitfulness). Her colour is emerald green.

POSEIDON

ARCHETYPE

Serious, mature, bearded man, enthroned on or beneath the waves.

PSYCHOLOGICAL EMPHASIS

The anima introvertedly expressed through the cyclothymic masculine mode (periodical swings of mood between excitement and depression).

THE MYTH

Although a member of the godly company of Olympus, Poseidon was always subject to his brother's sovereign authority. Naturally, the 'old man of the sea' complained from time to time, but having dominion over all waterways, as well as the oceans, provided him with ample opportunity to take his revenge. The stories of his nature and deeds emphasise the power of the element of water manifesting through the deep unconscious. The fact that his kingdoms were subject to the ultimate authority of Zeus, lord of air, however, seems to be the Greek way of saying that intellect is a stronger force than emotion, the head being a better judge than the heart.

Poseidon is sometimes shown riding in a chariot drawn by Tritons carrying conch shells, but in the more popular representation, his carriage is drawn by bronze-shod white steeds with golden manes. The white horse has always had connections with the sea, as we can see in the Celtic myths. In addition to the white horse, all marine life was sacred to Poseidon. His magical symbol is the Trident, and his colour is coral.

ATHENE

ARCHETYPE

Invincible, but wise female warrior.

PSYCHOLOGICAL EMPHASIS

The animus extravertedly expressed through the active feminine mode.

THE MYTH

We left Metis (see Zeus, page 21) at the point where she and her unborn child had been swallowed by Zeus. Shortly after this unfortunate episode, the Father of the Gods was afflicted with a dreadful headache and sought the help of Hephaestus (or Prometheus according to some sources) who split his skull with a bronze axe to relieve the pain. As the wound opened, out sprang Athene shouting a triumphant cry of victory, fully armed and brandishing a sharp spear. Both Heaven and Earth were struck by the miracle, and the 'bright-eyed goddess' assumed a special place in all hearts.

Athene was a warrior goddess *par excellence*. So flawless was her strategy that not even Ares, god of war, could match her in battle. She wore a golden helmet and over her shoulder was slung the aegis that no arrow could pierce, fashioned from the skin of Goat Amaltheia. The finished product came in the form of a breastplate or cuirass, fringed and bordered with snakes, with the horrifying head of the Gorgon in the centre.

In the Trojan wars she sided with Greece and eventually entered into the affray herself, felling the mighty Ares with a single blow from her magic spear. She also patronised heroes, protected the brave and valiant and many were the favours she conferred upon Hercules during the period of his trials.

Athene was essentially a virgin goddess – some achievement among the Don Juans – both mortal and immortal – of the time. She was also highly skilled in certain domestic crafts, notably weaving and embroidery, was believed to bestow healing and health and is credited with inventing the flute. Her emblems were the owl, olive tree, helmet, spear and shield. Her colour is red-gold.

HERMES

ARCHETYPE

Slim, athletic man. Celestial messenger, herald to the gods. Patron of travellers.

PSYCHOLOGICAL EMPHASIS

The anima extravertedly expressed through the communicative masculine mode.

THE MYTH

The Olympian personality of Hermes was said to have been borrowed from an old Pelasgian divinity greatly honoured by Arcadian shepherds as a deity of movement, action and the element of wind or air. All kinds of profit – lawful and unlawful – came under his rulership, as well as games of chance. With the growth of the Olympian pantheon the story was that Zeus begat Hermes by the nymph Maia, daughter of Atlas, and, as one of the Olympians, Hermes assumed the role of patron of travellers and herald to the gods. Travel, commerce, learning, agility and all forms of mental activity were his forte and the delicate missions he undertook called for more than a hint of diplomacy and tact.

In his role as divine messenger he appeared to assume certain qualities associated with Biblical angels. He is usually depicted carrying a caduceus, the insignia of the medical profession, symbolising the balance necessary for good health and well being on the one hand and the chaos/order principle on the other.

He is credited with the invention of the lyre, which he gave to Apollo in exchange for the caduceus, along with some sheep he had supposedly stolen from the sun god. This story is said to exemplify the natural powers of healing, as epitomised by the solar nature of Apollo, passing from the instinctive therapeutic mode to the logical and reasoning approach of clinical medicine. The Hippocratic Oath, however, which was (and in some cases still is) taken by members of the medical profession for centuries to observe a code of medical ethics, derived from that of the Greek physician Hippocrates (460–377 BC), commenced with the words, 'I swear by Apollo Physician, Asclepius ...', etc., with no mention of Hermes. (Of Asclepius, Apollo's physician son, we shall be hearing more in a later chapter.)

Hermes' symbols are the caduceus, petasus (winged helmet) and talaria (winged sandals). His colour is silver.

ARTEMIS

ARCHETYPE

Olympian virgin huntress.

PSYCHOLOGICAL EMPHASIS

The animus introvertedly expressed through the athletic feminine mode.

THE MYTH

Twin sister of Apollo, Artemis was goddess of the chase and of forests. Because the bear is one of her symbols, she is often confused with Callisto and, as was the case with the Egyptian Horus, there were several earlier goddesses who bore her name, notably the fertility goddess of Ephesus, with whom the Greek Artemis should not be confused.

Artemis was worshipped as an agricultural deity in Arcadia and some authorities connect her with the Celtic goddess, Berne, whose symbol was also a she-bear. Kerenyi asserts, however, that she was originally depicted as a lioness. Her brother, Apollo, is always seen in the solar context and, as a consequence, his sister became associated with the Moon. As she is frequently portrayed carrying a torch, which is more a solar than a lunar symbol, the superimposition or infusion of another archetype is suggested.

The story of the birth of Artemis and Apollo goes as follows. Leto, daughter of Croeus and Phoebe, was pursued by the Father of the Gods by whom she became pregnant. Upon hearing of her husband's indiscretion Hera was so enraged she decreed that Leto could only

Ancient depiction of Artemis as Winged Goddess with hunting lion

give birth at a place where the sun's rays never penetrated. In order that this command should not be disobeyed, Poseidon raised the waves like a dome over Ortygia, at the same time anchoring it to the depths of the sea with four pillars. Hera did everything she could to delay the birth by keeping Ilythia, goddess of childbirth, out of the way. For nine days and nine nights Leto suffered atrociously. Finally Iris was sent from Olympus to fetch Ilythia for her, and Leto was able to give birth first to Artemis, who was born on the sixth day of the month of Bysios, and then Apollo who was born on the seventh. Because of the difficulties her mother encountered prior to and during the birth of the twins, Artemis was designated patroness of childbirth.

Shortly after her birth Artemis approached her father with requests for eternal virginity, a bow and arrow like Apollo's, the office of bringing light and a saffron hunting tunic, which Zeus was happy to grant. Animals were sacred to her, but she had little time for people and severely punished those who made a nuisance of themselves or refused to abide by the laws of her domains. One of the translations of her name is said to mean 'safe and sound', or, 'she who heals sickness'.

Another gentle trait in her character was a love of music. She had a beautiful singing voice and as *Artemis hymnia* would sing to her brother's accompaniment on the lyre.

Both Apollo and Artemis were skilled in marksmanship, the esoteric meaning of which implies hunting for souls rather than the slaughter of animals, the 'prey' representing a spiritual goal. The bow and arrow therefore carry a profound metaphysical significance, being representative of the positive and negative aspects of the personality, or the anima/animus that need to be stretched to their finest tension before the 'target' can be hit.

As with all the Olympian deities, it would be impossible to do justice to her history and deeds in so brief a synopsis, but Artemis' connection with the Egyptian cat goddess, Bast, needs some explanation. A myth tells us that when the Greek gods fled into Egypt, hotly pursued by the monster Typhon, Artemis changed herself into a cat and, in this form, took refuge in the moon. One Egyptian rock temple dedicated to Bast was called *Speos Artemidos*, 'The Cave of Artemis'.

Like Athene, Artemis was a virgin goddess and she showed no mercy to anyone who attempted to disregard her vow. Legend has it that only once did she fall in love and that was with Orion, the hunter, but Apollo became jealous of his sister's affection and tricked her into accidentally shooting the object of her love. Both children loved their mother and spared no effort to protect Leto in times of danger and distress.

Artemis' symbols are the bow and arrow (which she shared with her brother), and all animals, although the hind, dog, bear, cat and lion are usually associated with her. Her colour is amethyst.

APOLLO

ARCHETYPE

Beautiful golden-haired god of light, music, healing and prophecy.

PSYCHOLOGICAL EMPHASIS

The anima extravertedly expressed through the artistic masculine mode.

THE MYTH

Apollo is one of those gods who appear to have equivalents in several other pantheons. He could therefore be said to resemble the Norse Baldur, the Celtic Lugh of Llew and the Egyptian Horus, to name but three.

Apollo

He was, above all things, a god of light. After his birth (see Artemis, page 26), the island of Ortygia was renamed Delos, 'the brilliant', and because he was born on the seventh, that number became sacred to him.

Apollo, the celestial archer whose arrows were infallible, was the god of musicians, patron of prophecy, divine physician and representative of all forms of art and beauty. He was also known to patronise the sciences upon occasions, but more as an interested party than a technician. His famous retinue consisted of the Muses, who were nine in number: Clio, muse of history, Euterpe, patroness of the flute, Thalia, patroness of comedy, Melpomene, muse of tragedy, Terpsichore, mistress of lyric poetry and the dance, Erato, muse of erotic poetry, Polyhymnia, originally muse of heroic hymns but later designated muse of mimic art, Urania, muse of astronomy, and Calliope, senior of the nine muses, who was honoured as mistress of heroic poetry and eloquence.

Apollo is credited with inspiring the famous maxims that were carved in the porch of his temple: 'Measure in all things', 'Know thyself' and 'To commit oneself is to court misfortune'. His symbols are the lyre, bow and arrow, dolphin and all divinatory aids. His colour is yellow-gold.

DEMETER

ARCHETYPE

Beautiful, but grave mature woman. Goddess of fertility. Patroness of the Mysteries.

PSYCHOLOGICAL EMPHASIS

The anima introvertedly expressed through the maternal mode.

THE MYTH

As goddess of the soil and all growing things, Demeter had much in common with the old mother goddesses Gaia and Rhea, her name being derived from the root words for 'earth' and 'mother', which naturally connect her with the underworld and all growing things issuing from the soil.

In Arcadia she was depicted with a horse's head and bearing in one hand a dolphin and in the other a dove. The Greeks equated her with the Egyptian Isis, but she would appear to have more in common with the Celtic horse goddesses Epona and Rhiannon.

Demeter's temples, called 'megara', were often found in forests and became associated with secret rites, while the famous Eleusinia were, of course, her mysteries (see Chapter 6). It is in her maternal aspect, however, that she is probably best known, appearing as a rather sad-looking, golden-haired lady, crowned with ears of corn or a ribbon and holding either a sceptre, ears of corn or a torch.

The story of Demeter and Kore, her beloved daughter, constituted the basis for the Eleusinian mysteries. According to the myth, Hades, brother of Zeus, snatched Kore while she was out picking flowers one day and claimed her as his bride – Zeus having apparently given his permission for this deed. Many were the trials of poor Demeter while she strove to regain her daughter and, because of her distress, she withdrew her energies from the earth so that nothing would grow. Both gods and men pleaded with her to restore her bounty, but Demeter was adamant – she would not permit the earth to bear fruit until she was reunited with her daughter. Zeus eventually sent Hermes to Hades with a request to return the maiden, who had been renamed Persephone. Hades grudgingly complied, but managed to persuade her to eat a few pomegranate seeds, the symbols of marriage, beforehand thus sealing the union. When once again she was back in her mother's arms, Demeter questioned her as to whether she had eaten any food while in Hades' domains because, 'If thou hast not eaten thou shalt live with me on Olympus. But if thou hast, then thou must return to the depths of the Earth'.

Much to Demeter's chagrin, poor Persephone admitted to eating the pomegranate seeds, but, as a compromise, Zeus decided that Persephone should dwell one-third of the year with her husband and the remaining two-thirds with her mother. Demeter settled for this bargain and once again the Earth produced fruit in abundance and all things flourished.

Before returning to Olympus, Demeter taught her divine science to the leaders of men, thus initiating them into her sacred mysteries. Demeter's symbols are the ear of corn and the torch. Her colour is cornflower blue.

ARES

ARCHETYPE
Tough, macho, strong, but insensitive, god of war.

PSYCHOLOGICAL EMPHASIS
The animus extravertedly expressed through the masculine warrior mode.

THE MYTH

The Greek Ares was not the nicest of characters. In addition to having a predilection for combat, he also had a very nasty temper and his squires, Deimos, Phobos and Eris (fear, fright and strife), hardly endeared him to people.

Inasmuch as he represented blind and uncontrolled passion, Athene was his natural enemy. Because her martial skills were coupled with wisdom and intelligence, the surly warrior had little chance against her in battle. Needless to say, Ares was not the happiest of lovers either. Although he managed to interest Aphrodite on the odd occasion, he was caught in the act by her husband, Hephaestus (a tale shortly to be told). Aphrodite bore Ares a daughter, Harmonia. This can be read as an indication that love can tame force and bring harmony.

Ares is usually depicted as a burly warrior, wearing a crested helmet. His symbols are all weapons of war and his colour is scarlet.

APHRODITE

ARCHETYPE

Beautiful, fair-haired, seductive love goddess.

PSYCHOLOGICAL EMPHASIS

The anima extravertedly expressed through the courtesan, or, 'hetaira' mode.

THE MYTH

Although Homer describes Aphrodite as the daughter of Zeus and Dion, the more popular view was that she was conceived in the foam of the ocean from the seed of Uranus, dropped there when he was castrated, her name meaning 'foam-born'. Even the Greeks admit that she is not exclusively theirs as she was also worshipped elsewhere under such names as Astarte, Ashtaroth and Ishtar. Each pantheon appears to have a representation of the love principle, and it is generally believed that because this principle was so strongly acknowledged by the people of ancient Greece, a character had to be built up around it.

Aphrodite was the classic, beautiful woman – fair-haired, blue eyed, voluptuous, Jung's 'Eve', the temptress and archetypal sex symbol.

In the context of the myths she was capable of arousing desire in anyone in whom it pleased or amused her to so do. With the exception of Athene, Artemis and Hestia, all gods, heroes and mortals yielded to her power, although on occasion she received a dose of her own medicine, as with the Anchises episode. As a punishment for distracting his divine mind, Zeus caused the goddess to fall blindly in love with a mortal man, the shepherd Anchises. After a blissful night together, Aphrodite appeared to Anchises in all her divine splendour. Being fully aware that any man who has lain with an immortal goddess would be stricken with premature old age, the shepherd was filled with terror, but Aphrodite reassured him and promised him a god-like son, asking him only that the name of the child's mother should never be revealed.

Aphrodite also possessed practical domestic skills, but it was decreed on Olympus that she should not make use of them as her talents were better employed in the arts of love.

The goddess of love had her own retinue – Eros and the Graces. The former was said to be her son, possibly by her husband Hephaestus or by Ares or even by Zeus. General opinion, however, tends to view Eros as epitomising the erotic principle. The Graces, who were three in number, had been fathered by Zeus on the Oceanid Eurynome. These were happy, pleasant divinities whose presence spread joy, sweetness and charm. Although given many names by earlier writers, they are generally accepted as being Aglaia, Euphrosyne and Thalia. They were portrayed as beautiful young women who served the goddess, attending to her toilette and adorning her for special occasions. The Graces were probably nature deities, originally associated with the spring and summer. Aglaia was called 'the brilliant', Euphrosyne, 'she who rejoices the heart' and Thalia, 'she who brought flowers'.

Aphrodite's famous attribute was her girdle, or, 'zona' and her colour is turquoise blue.

HEPHAESTUS

ARCHETYPE

Short, swarthy, broad-shouldered smith.

PSYCHOLOGICAL EMPHASIS

The animus introvertedly expressed through the artisan mode.

THE MYTH

Smith gods appeared in the pantheons of most of the early cultures. Agni was the Vedic god of fire, Britain had its Wayland, Egypt its Ptah, and so forth. There is a gnomey quality about Hephaestus that brings him in line with those archetypes who are rather unprepossessing in appearance but highly gifted.

According to Homer, Hephaestus was actually born lame, although other sources insist that, as the son of Hera and Zeus, he was so ugly at birth that his mother threw him from Olympus. Fortunately, he landed in the sea where he was rescued by Thetis and Eurynome who cared for him until he was strong enough to make a life for himself. He rewarded them with beautiful jewellery that he made with his own hands. When news of his skills reached his mother she made haste to fetch him back to Olympus where she set him up in a finely equipped smithy and gave him the beautiful Aphrodite for a wife.

Evidence for the physical problems associated with smith gods has recently been brought to light by archaeologists. Apparently the Bronze Age smelters as far back as 3500 BC knew that arsenic added to metal alloys made them much more durable and they maintained the optimum content of 2.5 per cent with great accuracy. The use of this metal was later phased out, however, on account of its side-effects (fragility and breaking of the bones of the legs and feet), which constituted health hazards for those who made it. Thus it is little wonder that smith gods are usually depicted as lame.

All the gods and goddesses had recourse to Hephaestus' skills at one time or other, his craftsmanship being unquestionably the best there was around Olympus or anywhere else for that matter. The beautiful and useful objects he made included Zeus' golden throne, sceptre and thunderbolt (although, according to some authorities the gifts of thunder and lightning were bestowed upon Zeus by the Cyclopes in gratitude for his liberating them from their imprisonment by his grandfather, Uranus), the arrows of Apollo and Artemis, Helios' winged chariot, Demeter's sickle, Hercules' cuirass and, of course, Pandora. He also constructed a set of golden mechanical female androids, as well as some three-legged robot tables to help him in the more menial tasks in his smithy.

Hephaestus is probably best known, however, for his famous net. Suspecting his wife of infidelity, he forged a net so fine that it could not be seen, but so strong that it could not be broken. One evening, as Aphrodite shared her couch with Ares, Hephaestus stole up on the couple and waited for them to fall asleep, whereupon he spread the net over them and invited the whole company of Olympus to come and witness how he had been betrayed. Zeus finally persuaded him to let them go after extracting a promise from Ares to pay the price for his adultery. From the attitudes adopted by the Olympians who were obliged to witness the incident, one rather suspects that the Greeks were pointing out the folly of washing one's dirty linen in public.

Hephaestus' symbols are the hammer and tongs, conical bonnet and net. His colour is bronze.

HESTIA

ARCHETYPE

Gentle, reserved maiden lady.

PSYCHOLOGICAL EMPHASIS

The animus introvertedly expressed through the self-effacing feminine mode.

THE MYTH

Hestia was one of the older goddesses, being the sister of Zeus, Demeter, Poseidon and Hera. Her name means 'hearth', or, the place in the house where fire burned, the food was cooked and from which warmth and comfort were derived. Fire was very important to primitive people as it provided a dialogue between men and the gods via the sacrificial flame.

Hestia's origins are obscure and neither Homer nor Hesiod appear to be familiar with her. She was essentially a virgin goddess who chose a modest existence in spite of the splendours of Olympus. Her character was one of reserved dignity and repose that served to contrast her with the more robust and flamboyant female Olympians. Although unmarried herself, Hestia protected the hearth and home, ensuring continuity and stability therein.

Hestia's symbols are the flaming circle, veil and domestic hearth or fireplace. White is her colour.

New pantheons were usually formed from the remnants of older ones and the 12 Olympians were no exception, having been woven from the fabric of earlier themes and fashioned by those cultures that affected the prevailing influences of the times. A healthy enquiry into the psychology of those who accepted and propagated them can afford the occult seeker a fair degree of insight into the archetypal manifestations appropriate to the period in world history, general evolutionary trends, and contributory imprint on the ethos in question.

Without a shadow of doubt, civilisation over the centuries after classical Greek times owed much to the cultural, logical, magical (albeit hidden) influences of the inhabitants of Mount Olympus and their creators.

4·SUBSIDIARY DIVINITIES AND OTHER MYTHOLOGICAL PERSONAE

In addition to the 12 Olympians, there were several other gods and godlings who were important in the Greek mystical and magical scene, and who would also appear to carry psychological connotations as far as the human condition is concerned. The following represent those that bear the strongest influence.

HADES

As has already been mentioned, Hades – also known as Pluto, from the Greek 'plouton', meaning wealth or riches, alluding to the treasures to be found deep within the earth itself or the money to be made from the raw materials mined from the earth, chose not to dwell on Olympus with his brother, preferring his own underworld regions in which he was absolute master. He did surface on two occasions, however. First, to abduct Persephone and, second, to seek healing for a wound inflicted upon him by Hercules. He wore a helmet that rendered him invisible, so if and when he did choose to visit Earth, no one would observe his presence and he could move around without being discovered.

Hades' Underworld associations are indicative of the lower nature, id, shadow or those baser instincts that lie dormant in civilised society until such times as they are encouraged to surface by the group or collective. This can be seen in revolutionary group or mob situations, when the process of mass dehumanisation gives birth to the group entity and the submerging of the individual. Families, friends, people who have been known, loved and respected for years suddenly become 'the enemy', because they appear to be on the opposite side. Politics and religion have been noted dehumanisers and depersonalisers. It is worth bearing in mind that just as we each have our personal shadow, groups or collectives also acquire a shadow identity that assumes the colour or emphases predominant in the shadows of its members.

Hades was often invoked by the Greeks as the giver of wealth, but, as in the case of all Underworld divinities or demons, there was always a price to be paid for his services that, as the collector of souls, he had no difficulty in extracting sooner or later.

His symbols are the Helmet of Invisibility and the cypress tree.

PERSEPHONE

The story of Persephone has already been related in detail in Chapter 3 (see Demeter, page 30) and although this would appear to be limited to a single episode, the psychological implications of the archetype are highly informative. Persephone lived one-third of the year with her husband and the remaining two-thirds with her mother on Olympus. In psychological terms, she literally lived in two worlds and, although the major portion, as represented by the two-thirds above ground, were experienced in 'consciousness' as we might know and recognise it, the remaining third saw her chained to her role as queen of her husband's subterranean regions – the unconscious or subconscious mind. The Persephone syndrome could be seen as analogous to the awake/sleep states.

I have recently heard the Persephone archetype likened to the natures of the astrological dual signs – Sagittarius, Pisces and Gemini – although my own experiences and observations incline me to favour the latter. I have known several Geminis who have been able to live in two situations at the same time – both of which were totally detached from each other – without suffering the sort of anxiety neurosis or psychological fragmentation that might have afflicted those born under other signs. Persephone is also seen by some psychologists as another manifestation of the cyclothymic personality, although the earthy nature of the archetype inclines those who are working through it to make a more profitable job of their creative talents than their more watery (Poseidonian) brethren.

Persephone's symbols are the pomegranate, bat and narcissus.

HECATE

Originally a Thracian Moon goddess, Hecate is often confused with Artemis as her name is said to derive from the feminine form of one of the titles of Apollo – the 'far-darter'. She is usually considered as the third member of the triple Moon goddess unit, or, Crone, Artemis being the maiden and Demeter the mother (or Aphrodite, the nubile woman, depending on the specific triplicity). Her power embraced both the sky and the Earth and the gifts she bestowed included wisdom, victory and, as would naturally be expected of a goddess of the Underworld – wealth.

The Crone aspect of the Triple Goddess is believed to relate to the intuitive facet of the mental trinity – that side of our nature that only comes into focus with the maturity of advancing years. The other two aspects are the instinctive (maiden), intimating that in our youth we are guided to a great degree by our feeling nature and the rational – which predominates those middle years during which we are usually struggling to make a living and coping with the contingencies of everyday life.

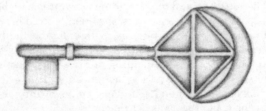

Key of Hecate
(combining crossroads theme and last phase of the Moon)

Always the ally of Zeus, Hecate was greatly respected on Olympus, although it did not appear to be her lot to dwell there. One legend tells how she incurred Hera's wrath by stealing her make-up to give to Europa. In fleeing to Earth to escape the punishment of the Mother of the Gods, Hecate sought shelter in the house of a mortal woman who had just given birth to a child, a contact that rendered Hecate impure. So that her pristine state could be restored, the Cabeiri escorted her to Acheron and henceforth she became a divinity of the Underworld.

As Peytania, queen of the dead, her connections were decidedly magical. Purifications, expiations, enchantments and all magical charms came under her aegis, while hauntings – of both the pleasant and unpleasant varieties – were attributed to her and her minions. Her most frequent visitations took place near burial places and scenes of crimes and triple-faced figures of the goddess were frequently found at crossroads and honoured on the eve of the full Moon. In fact, the crossroad maintained its sinister reputation for many centuries, the bodies of suicides and violent criminals being buried there in the hope that Hecate would find them quickly and despatch them hastily to her domains, thus allaying the chances of them causing problems for the living. During her nocturnal wanderings she was accompanied by a pack of infernal hounds, which is reminiscent of the Hindu goddess Kali.

Hecate's symbols are the dog and the key.

DIONYSUS

Semele, daughter of King Cadmus of Thebes, caught the amorous eye of Zeus who proceeded to woo her in disguise. Hera, however, determined to throw the proverbial spanner in the works, disguised herself as a nurse and slyly suggested to Semele that she request her lover to appear to her as he really was, for how else could she be sure that he was not, in fact, some dreadful monster?

Realising the destructive effect such a manifestation would have on the object of his passion, Zeus begged Semele not to ask such a favour of him, but she was adamant, and the Father of the Gods was compromised into a position where he was obliged to keep his word and display his full radiance. Being unable to endure such dazzling fire, Semele was immediately consumed and the child she carried in her womb would also have perished were it not for a thick shoot of ivy that miraculously created a green screen between the unborn babe and Zeus' celestial light. Gathering up the infant, Zeus enclosed it in his own thigh and, when its time was come, he drew it forth with the aid of Ilythia. Thus Dionysus was born.

Zeus made several more attempts to shield the godling from Hera's wrath, during which those who aided his efforts were severely punished by Hera, usually by being driven mad. When Dionysus reached manhood, Hera imposed a similar fate on him. Consequently, he spent the ensuing years roaming the world in the company of his tutor, Silenus, and a band of wild satyrs, maenads and other fabulous beasts. After many years of wandering, plunder, destruction and suffering, Dionysus finally regained his sanity, was established as divine and welcomed into Olympus by his father.

The popular interpretation of this legend concerns the spread of the vine cult across Europe, Asia and North Africa, with its attendant side-effects and, no doubt, many of the monstrous beasts who accompanied Dionysus during his period of madness could be equated with the delusions of inebriation. However, the 'twice-born' inference implies the transformation principle, while also according

Dionysus with his alter-ego the child Iachos

with those rites of maturation (rebirth) that constituted part of the ceremonials of many a primitive tribe. It is also re-echoed in Christian baptism and the rituals of several other major religions.

Periods of what the Greeks called 'madness' usually refer to those times in our lives when we seem to act out of character, throwing logic, reason and normal behaviour patterns to the winds. Episodes of exaggerated limerance (romantic love) are a classic example of this and, although there are many who manage to escape Aphrodite's girdle or Cupid's shafts, those of us who have fallen prey to them frequently feel rather embarrassed about it afterwards.

The character of Dionysus also has a prodigal son interpretation, in that it is representative of those people who have overcome either a severe cacoethes (uncontrollable urge or desire) or a weakness of character and emerged, albeit somewhat scarred, having transmuted their negative tendencies into a more disciplined mode. During the restructuring process the Dionysian person may descend to the depths of physical or even mental degradation only to rise from that abyss, to become a pillar of society.

Dionysus' symbol is the thyrsus, or, ivy-twined staff, surmounted with a pine-cone.

THEMIS AND NEMESIS

Themis was the Olympian goddess of Justice, or, celestial lawyer. We have already discussed her role in the life of Zeus, while another story tells how she made Apollo a present of the Delphic oracle that she had inherited from her mother, Gaia.

Themis' epithet, 'sotiera', suggests a protection of the just and punishing of the wicked, while, as a wisdom goddess, she was known as Euboulos, the good counsellor. Her task on Olympus involved maintaining good order, regulating ceremonial events and presiding over public assemblies.

Nemesis, we are led to believe, originated as a moral concept that was concerned with the inexorable equilibrium of the human condition. Man could displease the gods either by breaking moral laws or by acquiring so many worldly goods that these placed him in a position of mastery over his fellow men, both of which, it seems, incurred divine wrath. Later, Nemesis became a more defined divinity with her own genealogy. According to some she was the daughter of Oceanus while others claimed she had been born of Night and Erebus. Eventually, it was decided that Dike was her mother after which she became an equitable deity. She is frequently portrayed with a finger to her lips, which is said to suggest that silence is always advisable if one does not wish to court divine anger.

Certain homespun philosophies that have survived to this day appear to have origins in Greek legend, the Nemesis concept being a fine example. I have often heard the saying, particularly among the older generation and countryfolk that, 'God gets jealous if you have too much or love too deeply'. In fact, I can recall a particular case of a devoted couple in their early forties who lived for each other to the exclusion of all else. When the husband died suddenly and unexpectedly the villagers were heard to say, while sadly shaking their heads, 'They were too possessive of each other. No wonder God got jealous and split them up'. I have also heard a similar comment made about the very rich, especially when catalogues of their woes appear in the popular press.

The symbol attributed to Themis is the Scales of Justice, while Nemesis is accorded the apple bough, stag horn, wheel, silver bough and scourge.

HELIOS AND SELENE

Although Apollo was officially god of the solar light, the orb of the sun itself was accorded a separate divinity in the person of Helios. It is generally believed, however, that Helios was the solar divinity of an earlier pantheon, probably from another culture, who was conveniently incorporated into Greek mythology in much the same way that many Christian saints, St Brigid for example, were originally pagan deities.

Helios drove a chariot that was drawn by a team of magnificent white-winged horses whose names were Lampon, Phaeton, Chronis, Aethon, Astrope, Bronte, Pyroeis, Eous and Phlegon. Just as Helios guided his solar vehicle across the heavens from east to west, as her brother retired, Selene commenced her journey across the night sky. She did not always travel by chariot, however, as she was sometimes seen mounted on a horse or mule. The latter classifies her as a remnant of the old matriarchal days when horses were sacred to the Moon goddess.

Helios and Selene represent the 'lights' in astrology, their influences relating to natural forces rather than specific archetypes. Although nine names are given for Helios' steeds, he is traditionally shown in a chariot drawn by only four horses, representing no doubt, the quaternary principle. Selene also connects with the number nine, which was sacred to the Triple goddess in her Celtic mode, and the Qabalistic sphere of Yesod, Foundation (usually attributed to the Moon).

DIONE

Originally a Pelasgian divinity, Dione was the daughter of Oceanus and Tethys and, according to some sources, the mother of Aphrodite by Zeus. Her close association with Zeus may be evidenced in the functioning of the Dodona oracle, her priestesses apparently sharing the oracular gifts equally with the priests of Zeus. According to the Pelasgian creation myth, a Titaness of the same name was allotted joint rulership of the planet Mars with Crius, while a similar divinity also appears in Phoenician mythology. Whether there was any connection between these, however, we are not told.

I rather incline to the opinion that Dione was another name for the old Earth goddess, Rhea, whose oracle at Dodona was appropriated by Zeus when the Olympian pantheon officially took over. She therefore falls into the category of those goddesses who formed part of the Old Religion and, as such, her psychological connotations would accord with those of the Triple Goddess, probably in the Crone aspect.

ILYTHIA

At one time there were two Ilythia's, both daughters of Hera, who presided over birth and brought relief to women in labour pain. No child could be born without their presence and no mother could find relief without them. Although Artemis was later worshipped as goddess of childbirth, due to her own miraculous birth, she did not appear to interfere with the ministrations of these goddesses. Ilythia later acquired a single identity, but her archetype was probably carried over from pre-Hellenistic times and could be traced back to the Minoan or an earlier period.

Ilythia is usually depicted kneeling with a torch in one hand and the other extended in a gesture of encouragement.

IRIS

The sister of the Harpies and one of the Olympian messengers, Iris was the personification of the rainbow. In her divine form she appeared clothed in a long tunic, her hair was held by a bandeau and she carried a caduceus. Golden wings were attached to her shoulders and she was often depicted wearing winged sandals.

Although she served Zeus, Iris was devoted to Hera, and, in addition to carrying messages for the Mother of the Gods, she also effected Hera's vengeance. Noted for her caring qualities, which she dispensed to immortals and mortals alike, Iris was a much-loved divinity, which seems to be the old Greek sages' way of telling us that life's storms are frequently followed by a rainbow, from which illumination we may receive solace, good news and hope.

Her symbols are the rainbow and golden cup.

HEBE AND GANYMEDE

Hera's daughter Hebe was worshipped by the Greeks as a goddess of youth, as she personified the beautiful young maiden who never aged. The duties of divine cup-bearer were hers until she incurred her mother's wrath over some minor incident and was replaced by Ganymede. Hera finally stopped being angry with her, however, and when Hercules was eventually admitted to the Olympian company she gave him Hebe as his wife.

Ganymede was venerated at Sicyon and Phlius together with Hebe. He was depicted as a beautiful adolescent youth in a Phrygian cap and was sometimes carried through the air on the back of an eagle. Zeus was particularly struck by the youth's beauty and arranged for him to become his personal cup-bearer.

The psychological and magical message behind the nature of these godlings would appear to be that, while beauty of form and face might, at certain stages in our development, appear to aid our growth, they can also chain us to a life of service.

ZAGREUS

Prior to her abduction to the Underworld by Hades, Persephone gave birth to Zagreus, whose father was Zeus. The beings who guarded his cradle – the Curetes according to some legends and the Korybantes by other accounts – fell foul of Zeus' old enemies, the Titans, who came in disguise one night and stole the infant. In an effort to escape from them, Zagreus tried changing shape, becoming Zeus in a goatskin, Cronus as the raingiver, a lion, a horse, a horned serpent, a tiger and a bull. At this final point the Titans seized him by the horns and hastily dispatched him. Athene happened to witness this dreadful event and noticing that Zagreus' heart was still intact, enclosed it in a gypsum figure into which she breathed life so that he became immortal.

Zagreus' later association or possible identification with Dionysus is no doubt a throwback to the violent rites that were common to the cults of both godlings prior to the civilising influence of the philosophers, covering the body with gypsum often constituting part of the ancient mysteries of both initiation and rebirth.

PEGASUS

When the Gorgon Medusa, was decapitated by Perseus, the two children she had been carrying, who had been fathered by Poseidon – Pegasus, the winged horse, and Chrysaor, the golden warrior – sprang fully grown from her body. Both had been conceived, rather irreverently, in the temple of the goddess Athene, which gave considerable offence to that divine personage.

Pegasus was a gentle and beautiful creature. Although he appeared as a winged horse, he possessed many noble characteristics that could put men to shame.

The mortal Bellerophon, son of Glaucus, was asked to destroy the Chimaera, a fire-breathing she-monster. Before setting out on this mission he consulted Polyeidus, the seer, who advised him that its success depended on his catching and taming the fabled Pegasus. Bellerophon sought the beast and found him drinking quietly from a crystal pool. Using a golden bridle that Athene had conveniently presented to him, he was able to catch Pegasus, mount him and set off on his quest. So successful was this team of man and horse that Bellerophon's services as a hero were much sought after by mortals and immortals alike. One day, however, he overstepped the mark by presumptuously undertaking a flight to Olympus on the back of Pegasus. Affronted by such conceit, Zeus sent a gadfly that stung Pegasus under the tail, causing him to rear and send his rider tumbling to earth. Pegasus, however, completed the journey to Olympus where he was made welcome by all the gods.

This story is a shrewd illustration of the folly of assuming that something or someone is subject to our will and cannot function successfully without us. When it comes to the crunch, the boot often turns out to be on the other foot. I rather suspect the Greeks were also trying to tell us that being a member of the human race does not, in itself, warrant our acceptance into more transcendental realms. The fact that it was the horse who made it to Olympus and not the man is surely meant to convey something about our own status in the universal scheme of things.

A point of interest: Aquarius, ruler of the New Age, falls under the constellation of Pegasus. Perhaps during the ensuing epoch we are destined to witness the unfolding of a new awareness of some of the more misunderstood or rejected facets of existence external to our own environment, together with a spiritual acceptance of those other life forms with whom we share the planet Earth.

THE MUSES

These nine supernaturals formed the retinue of Apollo. They varied in number from time to time, however, and we are told that there were originally only three of them. In Lesbos seven were acknowledged, while the Pythagoreans favoured eight. The numerology involved tells us something of their origins. Three and nine were essential lunar numbers associated with the Triple Goddess, while the eight has masonic connotations and accords with the cult of reason rather than the more instinctive goddess religions. The names of the nine muses and their attributes are given in Chapter 3 (see Apollo, page 29).

THE HORAE

The name 'Horae' signifies a period of time that may be applied to the year, season or hour. The Horae were meteorological divinities who showered the earth with rain, without which nothing could grow. Later they were said to preside over nature itself and the order of the seasons, but there was considerable confusion as to their true roles even in those far off times.

They varied in number, with the people of Athens favouring Thalio, the bringer of flowers and Carpo, who brought fruit. Hesiod counted three: Eunomia, who saw that laws were observed, Dike, who watched over justice and Eirene, who ensured a state of peace. On Olympus they were allotted special tasks, one of which was to guard the gates of Heaven. Eunomia, Dike and Eirene were the daughters of Zeus and Themis. They loved to dance and often accompanied the Graces to form part of Aphrodite's retinue. They were also the helpers of children and young people generally to whom they showed much tenderness and care.

THE GORGON

Not all the fabulous beasts or mythological supernaturals were gentle, loving creatures, however. There were also the 'nasties' to contend with. These were usually conglomerations of whatever the Greeks of those times saw as being ugly or horrendous. Many of the creatures of evil that the heroes were sent to dispose of represent aspects of the self that need to be faced up to and conquered: the Gorgon Medusa, for example.

Medusa was the only mortal of three horrendously ugly sisters, the daughters of Phorcys and Ceto, the other two being Sthena and Eurale. Medusa had serpents for hair, huge teeth, protruding tongue and a face so ugly that all who gazed at her were petrified with fright.

By coupling with Poseidon in Athene's own sacred temple, she incurred the wrath of Athene who sought to punish her by assisting the hero, Perseus, in his quest to slay her. First of all, the goddess showed the hero the images of the three Gorgons so that he could distinguish Medusa from her immortal sisters, at the same time cautioning him never to look at Medusa directly, but only at her reflection. Hermes also helped Perseus in his task by giving him an adamantine sickle, or, 'harpe', with which to decapitate the Gorgon.

The hero also needed a pair of winged sandals, a magic pouch or wallet in which to contain the head and the dark Helmet of Invisibility that belonged to Hades. These he was eventually able to obtain from the nymphs who guarded them, after which he fled west to the land of the Hyperboreans where he found the three Gorgons asleep. Fixing his eye on the reflection in the shield, and allowing Athene to guide his hand, Perseus cut off Medusa's head with a single stroke of the sickle, whereupon, to his amazement, the winged horse Pegasus and the warrior Chrysaor sprang fully grown from her dead body (see Pegasus, page 45). Without further delay, he thrust the head into his pouch and took flight – according to some authorities being borne aloft by Pegasus himself.

Medusa's ugly sisters attempted pursuit but were unable to see their prey, Hades' helmet having rendered him invisible. Perseus presented the head to Athene, who incorporated it into her protective armour as a defence against attackers, which is believed to represent the role played by the mind in overcoming the id, shadow or lower nature.

This is surely one of the most psychologically interesting of the heroic myths, the inference being that people often recognise and are annoyed by those very failings in others that they themselves are prone to. There is also a Medusa-like quality about mirror complexes in that the Gorgon could be seen to mirror the real self that cannot be faced, much like Dorian Gray's famous picture.

THE MOERAE, OR FATES

Homer saw these beings as representing man's individual and inescapable destiny – it was only Hesiod who treated them as minor divinities. Daughters of Night, these three, white-robed, grey-haired divinities were named Clotho, Lachesis and Atropos. Clotho, the spinner, personified the thread of life, Lachesis, the apportioner, often called 'chance' – that timely element of good luck that we all hope will make its presence felt at some point in our lives – and Atropos, who stood for those fatalistic conditions that are generally described as karmic.

The Moerae shadow the whole of a person's life. They arrive with Ilythia at the moment of birth and are present at the point of death when it is their duty to sever the cord of life. In ancient Greece they were also invoked at the time of marriage to ensure a happy and lasting union.

They dwelled on Olympus and submitted to the authority of Zeus, who commanded them to see that the natural order of things was respected. Their gift of prophecy manifested itself mainly at the time of birth, at which point they were able to behold the entire life of the newborn child.

It is interesting to view some of these old myths in the light of modern scientific knowledge. It is now known, for example, that our future health tendencies, as well as our psychological type and potentialities, are genetically preprogrammed prior to birth.

THE KERES AND ERINNYES

When it was destined that a person should meet with a violent or difficult end, this onorous task was executed by the Keres, who were sometimes referred to as 'the Dogs of Hades', intimating their association with Hecate. They did not undertake this work for the Moerae alone, however, being assisted by the Erinnyes.

This latter group of spirits were entrusted with the special mission of punishing the crime of patricide and the violation of oaths and promises. Here we are no doubt dealing with personifications of moral ideas or principles and the serious student should have no difficulty in effecting a distinction.

CERBERUS

According to one legend, Cerberus, the mighty watchdog who guarded the gates to Hades' Underworld had 50 heads and a 'voice of bronze', his parents being Typhoeus and Echidna. More generally, however, he is portrayed with three heads bristling with serpents. Either way he was a terrifying sort of character and once inside his gates there was little chance of escape. The gentle Orpheus managed to subdue him with music and sweet song, which was probably the early Greeks' way of telling us that the energies from our primordial past, which sometimes surface through our subconscious minds, are best tamed by gentleness and harmony.

Hercules' twelfth Labour consisted of fetching Cerberus from his subterranean portal to the world above and bringing him to the palace of Eurytheus as evidence of the fulfilment of his task, after which the hound was allowed to return to its own Underworld domains.

The dog archetype features in the mythological underworlds of many pantheons. The hounds of Hecate and Kali we have already considered: the Egyptians had Anubis as their psychopompous (conductor of the souls of the dead), Merlin his black dog and the Eskimos their goddess who shared a life of conjugal bliss with her dog husband at the bottom of the sea.

THE SIRENS

The word 'siren' comes from the Greek word meaning 'to bind or attach', which gives us a clear indication of the role played by these beings in human psychology. The three Sirens were named Thelxiepeia, the enchantress, Aglaope, she of the glorious voice, and Peisinore, the seductive.

They were the servants of Persephone in that they lured people to their doom and therefore added to the population and therefore the might of that goddess' domains. Originally winged, they were deprived of their flight after challenging the Muses to a singing contest that they lost, their effrontery having offended the god of music himself. Later, the bird imagery gave way to the fish's tail on a human torso, from which figure the traditional mermaid probably evolved.

In spite of their pernicious natures, however, they did not always win. Odysseus managed to overcome them by binding himself to the mast of his ship when passing their island, while his men had been instructed to fill their ears with wax so that they could not hear their seductive songs. What we are surely being told is that it is possible to socialise with people whom we know to be not altogether trustworthy, as long as we are not seduced by their soft words and sweet music.

THE NEREIDS

These 50 sea sprites were born to Nereus, the truthful, and Doris, daughter of Oceanus. They were fair-haired and beautiful and dwelt with their father beneath the ocean. Nereid sisters often made mythological news: Thetis, for example, who features in the life of

Zeus, and Galatea, whose escapade with Acis has been the inspiration for poetry and music down the ages.

THE NYMPHS

The Meliae, or, ash nymphs, were born from the spilled blood of Uranus. The term 'nymph', however, is employed in Greek mythology to cover a whole range of devas and not simply the Ondines, or, water spirits.

Nymphs were beautiful, youthful and charming. They inhabited the rivers and streams and kept watch on the forests and mountains. The Greeks gave them different names according to the regions with which they were associated. The Oreads were the spirits of mountains and grottos, the Nepaeae, the Auloniads, the Hylaeorae and the Alsaeids haunted the woods and valleys, while the Dryads were the forest or tree spirits. The Hamadryads were so closely associated with trees that they probably represented entities of the tree or vegetable evolutionary strain itself rather than elemental or devic protectors.

THE FOUR WINDS

Eos, the dawn, and Astraeus, the starry sky, had four sons: Boreas, the north wind, Zephyrus, the west wind, Eurus, the east (or southeast wind, sometimes known as Apheliotes) and Notus, the south wind. Many were the old myths about the power of the winds, especially as fertilising agents, but then one has to realise that the Greeks were nothing if not accurate observers of all natural movements and the effects these could have upon the lives of people. So it is little wonder that they treated the spirits of the winds with a degree of respect.

THE HARPIES

The Harpies also had air associations, but of a less pleasant nature. They represented storms and tempests, and ill-luck and hardship were usually the aftermath of their pranks. In later times they were portrayed as hags although this was not always the case. Natural forces, like any other form of pure energy, can appear constructive or destructive and the Greeks, in their vividly graphic personifications, drew clear distinctions between the two aspects.

THE SPHINX

Unlike its Egyptian namesake, the Greek Sphinx was anything but friendly. The daughter of Typhon and Echidna, she had a woman's head, lion's body, serpent's tail and eagle's wings. Sent by Hera to punish Thebes for displeasing the goddess, she settled on Mount Phicium, near to the city, and asked everyone who passed by to answer a riddle she had learned from the three Muses:

'What being, with only one voice, has sometimes two feet, sometimes three, sometimes four and is weakest when it has the most?'

Anyone unable to render the correct answer was immediately slain and devoured by her. One day Oedipus chanced along that road and guessed the answer:

'Man, because he crawls on all fours as an infant, stands firmly on his two feet in his youth and leans on a staff in his old age.'

Completely shattered by her defeat, the Sphinx threw herself from the mountain and was dashed to pieces in the valley below, whereupon Oedipus was acclaimed king.

The message here would seem to be that once man has recognised his weaknesses and strengths, he is then ready to despatch the evils of blind ignorance that have previously condemned him to captivity or death. The necessity for logic or reason would also appear to be implied.

In keeping with the philosophy and religion of most early races, the Greeks also paid due deference to the energies that animated river and stream, forest and cave, wind and fire. In the myths, names are accorded both to the group elemental soul and those spirits that emanated from it. However, we are only skirting the edges of this study so there is considerably more to be learned by those with the time, inclination and dedication necessary for its pursuit.

5·THE TUTORS

In classical mythology, both mortals and immortals were tutored by non-humans who often assumed the form of fabulous beasts, such as Silenus the satyr, Chiron the centaur or the goat-footed Pan. The Greeks obviously inherited this knowledge from an older race whose people were metaphysically aware enough to realise that our species is not supreme in the universe, there being other life forms outside of the Earth environment that may conceivably have a broader and less exalted view of the superiority of their race. Many occultists share the view that, prior to the onset of our spiritual blindness, mankind was able to communicate with life forms, minds or essences from other dimensions, many of which were certainly his intellectual equal, and more so in some cases. Let us then examine the magical and psychological influences and inferences behind the three best known of those non-humans who, according to the Greek sages, appeared as fountains of inner knowledge and skills.

SILENUS AND THE SATYRS

Believed by some authorities to represent elemental spirits of the forests and mountains, satyrs were but one of many groups of beings that were part-human and part-animal in form. They are described as having low foreheads, snub noses, pointed ears, hairy bodies, goats' tails and cloven hooves. The most famous of these was Silenus, whose name means 'moon man'. The *Larousse Encyclopedia of Mythology* (Hamlyn, 1959), however, designates the 'sileni' as a whole and separate species, being originally genii of the springs and rivers. Here though we shall leave Silenus in the traditional satyr form.

Silenus was also traditionally viewed as a loud, jovial, character with a taste for wine, who also possessed a never-ending stream of knowledge and innate wisdom that he saw fit to dispense on certain

Satyr

occasions, notably his encounter with King Midas when he expounded the Atlantis story in some detail. As tutor to Dionysus, Silenus accompanied his charge during the wild, mad days of the godling's initiations. Plato, however, felt no irreverence in comparing his master Socrates with Silenus, so why should such an ugly, old, ill-disciplined half-man command the respect of one of the world's greatest sages and philosophers?

Of course, as with all Greek magic and mysticism, there is an inner mystery involved – nothing ever being quite what it seems. It therefore befell the initiate to the Mysteries to discover the force behind the outer mask. Satyrs, centaurs, unicorns or winged horses may form part of a muddled unreality to some people, but, in another dimension, or parallel universe that co-exists simultaneously with and within our own, they are realities. Man may accidentally peer into these universes when seriously ill, in his 'cups' or under the influence of hallucinogenic drugs, because, on such occasions, the discarding of programmed conditioning allows the barriers to drop sufficiently for the veil to be temporarily drawn aside. Of course, what is seen by the uninitiated is not understood, so it is naturally placed in the category of delusion. Only through the initiatory process, during which the brain is programmed by the psyche to seek out, face and fully comprehend the nature of other universes, will the seeker meet, be embraced and taught by the Tutors.

The esoteric theory is that Silenus, like Chiron and Pan, simply reflects the mental conditions of his pupils, acting as a mirror in which we may confront the various aspects of ourselves. If, therefore, the pupil is a debauched, hedonistic inebriate, lacking in self-control, then that will be the guise in which we will view the tutorial principle to whom he looks for guidance, in much the same way that a rough, loutish person looks up to those who have gained some form of power by aggressive means.

CHIRON AND THE CENTAURS

Forming part of the cortege of Dionysus, the centaurs had the torso and head of a man while the remainder of their body was that of a horse. According to the *Larousse Encyclopedia of Mythology* (Hamlyn, 1959), the etymological meaning of the name 'centaur' is 'those who round up bulls', which doubtless originated in the practice of rounding up cattle on horseback in much the same way as it was done by cowboys in the wild west. Like their satyr friends, however, the centaurs were also known for their wisdom and knowledge.

The best known and most respected of this clan is undoubtedly

Chiron, who was renowned for his scientific knowledge and medical skills, in which he had reputedly been instructed by no less than the healing divinities Apollo and Artemis, the divine twins. Chiron, in turn, tutored Apollo's famous son, Asclepius, in the healing arts. Chiron was loved and respected by both mortals and immortals, Hercules, in particular, being one of his closer associates.

While carrying out his fourth Labour, Hercules accidentally

Centaur

wounded his friend with an arrow. Although the hero tended the wound under the master's instructions, he was unable to ease the centaur's suffering and Chiron, being immortal, was obliged to endure the pain from which only death could bring him relief. He therefore exchanged his immortality for the mortality of Prometheus, for which sacrifice Zeus placed him among the stars as the constellation of Sagittarius.

The metaphysical interpretation of this myth is that the inhabitants of this parallel universe, which our mortal eyes are as yet unable to behold, have entered a temporary stage of transition (death) in order to allow Prometheus to finish the task he commenced with his gift of fire. In other words, when man has learned to master the divine fire of creativity within his own soul, then will the world of Chiron be once more open to him. Until the return to such golden times, however, the privilege is reserved for those whose heroic deeds of self-discipline, love and universal understanding earn them the right to learn from Chiron and his ilk.

PAN

It is generally agreed that Hermes was the father of goat-footed Pan, but his mother is sometimes mentioned as being Dryope or the nymph Deneis or Penelope, wife of Odysseus, or even Rhea. The more convincing story, however, is that this benign and gifted deity was the product of a union between Hermes and Goat Amaltheia.

The Olympians exploited Pan just as we exploit Earth today. Apollo wheedled the art of prophecy from him and Hermes copied a pipe Pan had carelessly dropped, claimed it as his own invention and promptly sold it to Apollo.

Although he was considered divine, the story spread that Pan had died. It was told by an Egyptian sailor named Thamus, who claimed to have heard a spirit voice tell him to announce upon reaching Palodes, that the great god Pan was dead. What Thamus probably heard was the ceremonial lament 'The all-great-god Tammuz is dead!', which was ritually chanted at certain times of the year.

During Plutarch's time, in the second half of the first century AD, Pan was very much alive, with shrines, altars and caves dedicated to him being regularly frequented. To the Greeks of old, Pan was not so much a half-man, half-goat as an individuated nature force to which they could easily relate. He was never a vicious or sinister deity; quite the reverse, in fact, being a god of song, dance and merriment.

During the early days of Christianity, in an effort to suppress nature worship, the adherents of the Christian cult adopted the Pan figure to epitomise their concept of evil. This produced some unfortunate repercussions in the ensuing centuries when many innocent people were persecuted as devil worshippers simply because they possessed knowledge of herbs, healing and husbandry. Sadly, such ignorance still exists with many fundamentalist Christians believing Paganism or Wicca to be synonymous with Satanism.

However, the latter is actually a perversion of Christianity. In other words, one has to believe in the Christian concept in order to acknowledge the existence of Satan and debase Christian practices, and neither of these beliefs are involved in Paganism.

The new eco-awareness, however, is slowly opening the doors for Pan's return. We may refer to things 'green' in terms of Gaia, or, earth-consciousness, but whatever the tag there is plenty of evidence in this day and age to suggest that this benign Greek deity is far from deceased.

The role of each tutor accords with a different aspect of the human psychological economy. Pan governs our instincts, Chiron our logic and reasoning and Silenus our intuitive faculties. Parallels could also be drawn between youth, maturity and the wisdom that comes with age in the same way that the Triple Goddess has her Maiden, Mother and Crone aspects. Eric Berne, of Transactional Analysis fame, brought the whole concept up to date with his Child/Parent/Adult complex, which goes to show that there is really nothing new under the sun – each generation's interpretation of age-old truths being designed to suit the pervading ethos and prevailing needs of the time.

6·MYSTERIES AND SACRED RITES

The sacred rites that dominated Greek culture can be classified under three main headings:

- rites of frenzy or divine possession, which mainly fall into the Instinctive, Emotional or Severity Code categories (see *The Psychology of Ritual*)
- public rites, which usually involved the general populace at the Emotional or Instinctive level, while the Initiates negotiated their Mysteries within the context of the Intellectual and Contemplative Codes
- rites of purification and dedication, which may involve all or any of the ritual Codes.

RITES OF DIVINE POSSESSION

Although the frenzy element appears in many early rites, there were those specifically known for their orgiastic-ecstatic content. These formed part of the cults and attendant mysteries of Dionysus, Sabazios, Zagreus and Phrygian, or, Thracian Bacchus, Cybele and Ida's Zeus, which were subsequently appropriated by the Orphics. Towards the end of the sixth century BC, Dionysus had become the symbol of universal life in that he grew up, suffered, died and was reborn in new circumstances. With the advent of the philosophers, the violent elements of Greek ritual slowly receded, giving way to a more sublime approach to the gods.

In Euripides' *Cretans*, the chorus of Bacchants are credited with the following song:

> Purity has been the law of my life from the day when I was initiated into the Mysteries of Ida's Zeus; when I took part in the sacrifices according to the rule of Zagreus, the lover of nocturnal journeys, lit torches in honour of the Great Mother and received the double name of Curetes and Bacchant. Clothed in pure white garments, I flee from the birth of mortals; I do not approach graves, and I do not tolerate in my food anything which has lived.[1]

Note the allusion to vegetarianism, a far cry from the description by Prudentius (AD 1011–50) in his *Peristephanon* in which he describes the initiation into the mysteries of Cybele (The Taurobolium) when the sacrificing of the sacred bull in all its gory detail appeared to offend the writer as much as it would most civilised people today since he ended his report with the comment,

> Afterwards, the flamens draw the corpse, stiffening now that the blood has gone forth, off the lattice, and the pontiff, horrible in appearance, comes forth, and shows his wet head, his beard heavy with blood, his dripping fillets and sodden garments.
>
> This man, defiled with such contagions and foul with the gore of the recent sacrifice, all hail and worship at a distance, because profane blood and a dead ox have washed him while concealed in a filthy cave.[2]

(NB: The consecrated priest emerging from the blood bath had embodied the divine essence and is therefore worshipped.)

Euripides' *The Bacchae* gives a wordy account of an attack by the Bacchae as described by one of the herdsmen to Penteus, the king of Thebes. This is too long a poem to repeat in full so I have chosen the following short extract, which highlights the horrendous and frenzied nature of these rites:

> Unarmed they swooped down upon the herds of cattle grazing there on the green of the meadow. And then you could have seen a single woman with bare hands tear a fat calf, still bellowing with fright, in two, while others clawed the heifers

to pieces. There were ribs and cloven hooves scattered every-
where, and scraps smeared with blood hung from the fig
trees.[3]

How much of this we are to believe, however, is open to conjecture as
these activities were doubtless embellished over the years.

PUBLIC RITES

'The traditional festival of Dionysus', writes Plutarch, '. . . was
formerly a simple, popular merry-making. At the head of the procession a jar of wine and a vine tendril, then a goat, followed by a
basket of figs and finally the phallus'.[4] All quite harmless, fertility-
type celebrations.

The population of various villages would attend these festivities to
display the legendary phallus of the god and exchange jokes, which
some scholars see as forming the origin of Greek comedy. D'Aviella
views the Lenea, or, feast of the wine-press and the Eleusinian
Anthesteria, or, flower festival, which were celebrated in Athens in
honour of Dionysus, as merely a development of a truly Flemish fair
that had found its way to the sunny shores of Hellas. Nor is he alone
in this view, Dionysus being a comparative late-comer to the Eleusinian *dramatis personae*.

RITES OF PURIFICATION AND DEDICATION

As the seventh century BC neared its end, the influence of Asiatic
religions began to spread across Greece. The theme behind most of
these beliefs was concerned with a god who died in order to rise
again – Attis, Adonis, Sabazios, the sun-god of the Phrygians,
Zagreus, the Great Hunter of Crete, and so forth. The suffering of
Dionysus was celebrated with alternate mourning and festivity, a
practice that is calculated to render the participant susceptible to
auto-suggestion and/or frenzy/ecstasy, depending on the nature and
sublimity of the ensuing rites. Mostly, however, it was the orgiastic
aspect that received emphasis.

Some authorities assert that the idea behind these wild ceremonies
was the identification of Dionysus with the growth of vegetation that
follows the winter, the blood libations serving to stimulate the
sleeping nature spirits into further activity. The principle rites of
Dionysus were always celebrated between the winter solstice and the
spring equinox. In like manner, he was also believed to take over the
Delphic oracle during those times, when Apollo went on his regular

winter holiday. A similar arrangement was effected in Celtic mythology by the characters of Llew, the solar god, and Gwyn-ap-Nudd, ruler of the Underworld.

According to another source, however, the original Dionysian Mysteries were concerned with the re-enactment of the god's hapless adventures and eventual period of suffering. This naturally served to establish the mode of abandonment for which certain earlier aspects of the cult became famous. With the advent of the Pythagorean schools, however, a new, more spiritual quality slowly crept in.

THE SAMOTHRACIAN, BACCHIC, ELEUSINIAN AND ORPHIC MYSTERIES

The Mysteries constituted one of the most important features in Greek religious life – the Samothracian, Bacchic, Eleusinian and Orphic being the best known. Each mystery had its own sacred emblems and involved different sets of trials that varied according to the degree of the Initiate. The public rites carried none of the inner meaning, however, and simply provided the general populace with an excuse to let their hair down and have a generally good, if somewhat libidinous, time.

Samothracian rites centred around four mysterious deities: Axieros, the mother, her children Axiocersos, male, and Axiocersa, female, from whom sprang Casindis, the originator of the universe. The festival probably symbolised the creation of the world, its growth and ensuing harvests. Connected with this was the cult of Cybele, goddess of the Earth, the blood-letting rites of whose priests, the Corybantes, were mentioned earlier. The cult of Bacchus is believed by some to have been brought to Greece from Egypt by Melampus, but general opinion tends to credit it with oriental or northern origins.

Greatest of all the sacred rites of Greece was undoubtedly the goddess-orientated Eleusinia, based on the Demeter/Persephone drama, and also incorporating the characters of Asclepius and Dionysus, both of whom were believed to have visited the dark regions of Hades. Homer's celebrated 'Hymn to Demeter' makes no mention of Dionysus among the Eleusinian gods, however, which rather suggests that his cult probably originated elsewhere and was incorporated into the Lesser Eleusinia at a later date. Its origins are obscure although, as we have already discussed, it carries oriental overtones. The Victorian scholar, G. R. S. Mead was of the opinion that it contained both Chaldean elements and archaic Semitism and that the god was not Thracian in origin, as was generally believed, a view with which I am inclined to agree in the light of other myths.

THE 'DEATH AND RESURRECTION' THEME

Tales of Dionysus' riotous exploits in the company of a ribald band of nymphs, satyrs and Maenads are hardly suggestive of spiritual sublimities, but then frenzy and ecstasy have ever been but a hair's breadth apart. So when it came to a letting go of the ego, or transference of consciousness to the god-nature, the people of those times obviously related the qualities of their deity to their own personal preferences.

As the vine was sacred to Dionysus, the bulk of his followers, as with the Phrygian Sabazius, considered that drunkenness equated divine possession. In later times devotees likened the plucking, crushing and pressing of the grape to form a pleasing nectar to the progress of the soul, which is formed whole and then crushed and pressed into shape by the trials of its earthly adventures, eventually to re-emerge as a refined and useful intelligence. This analogy was seen in the life of Dionysus himself, whose purification by way of madness and suffering finally gained him admittance to Olympus. Perhaps the prodigal son aspect of Dionysus hints at some inner teaching that, no matter to what depths of degradation our errant steps may take us, there is always the light of knowledge and love to lead us back onto the straight and narrow path to the spiritual heights.

In the process of his redemption Dionysus undoubtedly suffered, but this is surely the price paid by anyone who abandons him or herself to pure hedonism, the ascent from the resulting abyss constituting a much harder climb than that endured by the meeker, more stolid person who has strayed little. Yet, it we are to heed either the myth of Dionysus or the words of the biblical parable, it would appear that, because the experiences undergone by the prodigal son were more comprehensive than those encountered by his cautious brother, the rewards were correspondingly greater. Divest this story of its materialistic connotations and we are left with something a little nearer the truth, which is probably that both contribute equally to the Creative Whole, all experiences being necessary to its continuing expansion. Another interpretation, which is favoured by many scholars of the period who are also believers, is that, by descending to the depths of Hades and savouring the nature of Death itself, one's fear of the unknown or afterlife is automatically lifted. This is as real today as it was in those ancient times. Clinical studies of near death experiences (NDEs) establish that, once the abyss has been crossed or the veil drawn aside, however briefly, all fears of the inevitable departure vanish, leaving those involved with a sense of inner peace and security.

GRAECO-ORIENTAL RITES

The inner rites of Eleusis were secret and their esoteric content therefore unknown. In fact, the disclosure of their secrets was, according to Athenian Law, punishable by death. Thus it is little wonder that we are left to piece together those fragments that have filtered down to us through the centuries. The outer or exoteric side of the Eleusinia is fairly well recorded, however, and, rather than repeat myself, I would refer the reader to Chapter 4 of *The Psychology of Ritual*, which details the progress of the ceremonial procession, the sacred objects involved, the priestly ranks and other details of magical significance.

Views regarding the meaning behind the Mysteries differ considerably. Goblet D'Alviella, who is by no means convinced of their deeper mystical content writes:

> Many scholars believe the highlight of the ritual to be in the mystical drama. This belief is wrong, in so far as it sees the nucleus of the Mysteries in the revelation of the adventures of Demeter and her daughter. The theme of Eleusinian drama was never esoteric. It is explained from beginning to end, not only in the Homeric Hymn to Demeter and in other poems – such as the now lost songs of Pamphos and Achilocus, which could possibly be called liturgical, but also in purely profane works such as the essays or poems which Apollodorus, Ovid, Claudius and Nonnus dedicated to the same topic, without incurring the slightest reproach for indiscretion. Even the variations on the legend which undoubtedly had their origin in the local Eleusinian traditions – such as the events connected with Demeter's stay in this city – had long since been absorbed into the foundation of Greek mythology. It is probable, though, that the presentation of the abduction and the return of Cora was shown in itself as magic which could influence the abundance of the harvest, or rather the success of the sowing.[5]

However, we are told that the heroes inevitably prepared for their great feats by fasting, meditation and contemplation of the mysteries, Hercules himself having been initiated into the higher mysteries of Eleusis prior to undertaking his 12 Labours. One is therefore inclined to feel that there was some secret, esoteric knowledge, the nature of which was so profound that it never received mention outside of the Initiated.

Hippolytus, who lived in Rome in the first half of the third century AD, definitely speaks of '. . . the Athenians initiating people at the Eleusinia and showing to the epoptai (initiates of the highest grade) that great and marvellous mystery of perfect revelation, in solemn silence, cut wheat'.[6] Hippolytus commences his statement by telling us that the Phrygians and later the Athenians considered the 'cut wheat' as a Mystery, while Attis is also called 'the verdant cut wheat'. It is questionable that the Athenians would have adopted this cut wheat theme from the Phrygians since they had little time for the Phrygian Mysteries, despising both their content and symbolism. Perhaps Hippolytus mixed the symbolism of the two cults, which is very easily done, even in today's occultism.

In contrast, Tertullian of Carthage (AD 160–220) claimed that it was the phallus and not the wheat that was shown to the epoptai, which does not accord with the feminine nature of these mysteries. In an attempt to harmonise these conflicting reports by the early Christian fathers, Magnien drew attention to the wheat as symbolising illumination and the phallus as representing regeneration, which would give the Mysteries points in common with the Isis-Osiris story of Egyptian myth.[7]

Clement of Alexandria (circa AD 150–221) commented freely on certain undesirable aspects of the Mysteries of Deo, 'Deo' being the poetic form of the name Demeter, although the learned Bishop does not state specifically that the said Mysteries are synonymous with those of Eleusis. The symbols quoted by Clement would appear to refer to the Phrygian cult – the drums, cymbals and bridal chamber being important impedimenta in Phrygian ritual.

Reference is also made to the story of Baubo, one of the aborigines of Eleusis, with whom Demeter stayed during the period of her wanderings, the others being Dysaulus, Triptolemos, Eumolpos and Eubouleus. The last three named were herdsmen, the progenitors of the Eumolpids and Kerykes who formed the priestly cast of Athens. Baubo, it seems, offered the goddess food and drink, which she declined, causing Baubo to believe that she had in some way offended the divinity. She therefore displayed her pudenda to the goddess, which seemed to appease her so that she then ate and drank the offerings. The Baubo legend is obviously founded on some ancient local matrist rite, which involved a form of sacred exhibitionism similar to that of the Sheela-na-gigs of Celtica.

After telling the story of Baubo, Clement also mentions the synthema (password): 'And the synthema of the Eleusinian Mysteries is as follows: "I fasted, I drank the kykeon; I took from the kiste; having done my task, I placed in the basket, and from the basket into the kiste ..."'[8] The kiste was a cylindrical box or chest in which were kept the hiera of the Eleusinian cult, the hiera being the cult's most sacred objects whose revelation completed initiation. Kykeon was the special potion of meal and water, seasoned with soft mint, with which Demeter broke her fast. A similar potion was eaten by the Initiates in commemoration of the act of the Goddess.

I could continue quoting scholarly conjectures *ad nauseam*, but the safe assumption is that the Greek rites, like those of many other early cultures, were composed of a hotch-potch of totemistic practices and ancient primitive ceremonies into which the occasional shaft of truth managed to penetrate. This was subconsciously recognised and followed by those whose soul-age rendered them sufficiently sensitive to perceive and acknowledge its purity and wisdom. Plato was just such a man, as was his master, Socrates, while Pythagoras, Hippocrates and other men of wisdom managed to sustain that essential combination of logic and intuition that is the hallmark of the mature soul to the benefit and enlightenment of those of us who are still learning from them.

THE HISTORY AND SIGNIFICANCE OF ORPHISM

Amongst the orgies, sacrifices and riotously overt devotionalism that dominated the Eleusinia, the balance was maintained by the emergence of small groups of women and men who gave themselves entirely to holy and disciplined living. These were known as the Orphics.

When Pythagoras established his famous school at Crotona, he did little more than refuel an existing tradition that had survived the centuries, in spite of the negative Dionysian traits that had pervaded the more popular or public Mysteries. G. R. S. Mead tells us that the Pythagorean schools were absorbed into Orphism, Plato continuing the work of the master, but adding to it the dimension of reason so that the truth behind the Mysteries could be more easily assimilated and its benefits made more readily accessible to the uninitiated.

To the suffering, passion and resurrection of Dionysus the Orpheun adepts added a new mysticism and the character of the god underwent a profound modification. Out went the wine, orgies, hedonism and delirium, and instead there emerged, in the words of Plutarch, '. . . the god who is destroyed, who disappears, who relinquishes life and then is born again'. In other words, Dionysus became, like the Egyptian Osiris and the Christian Jesus, the Risen One.

It would seem logical that the Orphic Mysteries were initiated by someone bearing that name, which calls for a consideration of the Orpheus legend, if only to supply clues as to the origin of the cult. Orpheus was a hero of Thrace, but, unlike the regular crop of Greek strongmen, he was not known for his exploits at arms. Being a son of

Apollo, he had inherited his father's talent for music to such a degree that when he sang and played the lyre, so sweet were his tones that the most savage beasts would lie gently before him. This talent he put to good use during his adventures with the Argonauts on their quest for the Golden Fleece. So powerful, in fact, was his music that even the inhabitants of the Underworld fell under its spell.

Orpheus was married to Eurydice, whom he loved above all else. One day, however, while fleeing from Aristaeus, his wife received a mortal wound from a serpent. Heartbroken, the bard descended into the infernal regions where he so charmed Hades and Persephone that they allowed Eurydice to return to him, but with one condition: at no point during the journey from death to life should he turn to look at his beloved.

Eurydice, being naturally delighted to see her husband once again, begged him to turn and face her. When he refused, she took it as a mark of rejection and informed Orpheus that unless he made this obvious gesture to reassure her of his continued affection she would assume that his love had died, in which case she would prefer to stay with Hades and Persephone. Being greatly moved by her impassioned plea Orpheus turned to her, an act which cost him his love for ever.

This kind of single-minded devotion was obviously not understood by the Thracian women of the time and legend has it that they tore him to pieces in their anger, casting his head and lyre into the river Hebrus. Later the head was seen to be caught between some rocks where, for a long time, it delivered oracles. This story is reminiscent of other myths, notably the Celtic tale of Bran, whose decapitated head was also renowned for its prophecies, while the idea of being torn into pieces and reassembled according to a new and more enlightened design is totally Shamanic. There are other legends concerning the ultimate fate of Orpheus, but who he was and whether, in fact, he ever actually existed is open to conjecture.

Taking this story into account, the fact that the Orphic cults carried strong musical connotations is hardly surprising. At first glance Orpheus and Dionysus would appear to be strange bedfellows – almost opposites – the one representing the faithful lover and gentle musician whose power lies in the manipulation of harmonious sounds, while the other, as god of wine and abandonment, appears initially in a less favourable light. Surely the Mysteries are telling us that, although wine may loosen the mental barriers between the material and subtle worlds sufficiently for us to become aware of their existence, if we are to negotiate them successfully, it is rather via the path of suffering that we will eventually gain sufficient mastery of the 'self' to secure us a safe passage through altered states of consciousness – without the need for recourse to the fermented juice of the grape. Orpheus, on the other hand shows us an alternative way through beauty, art, gentleness and fidelity. Yet, in spite of his basic goodness, he too was obliged to descend to Hades (face his own unconscious) and suffer the loss of that which he loved the most. Dionysus is surely the god within us trying to grapple with weaknesses of the flesh, while Orpheus represents our more gentle traits that we may develop should we feel so inclined.

Orphic rites therefore consisted of a mixture of the attributes of both Orpheus and Dionysus. From the Orphic influence there came the music, while the unbridled rites of earlier Dionysiac cults gave way to the disciplined movements of the ritual dance.

I am often asked whether these rites could have a place in modern society, to which the answer must obviously be 'yes', if they are treated with the discipline and respect accorded to them by Pythagoras. There are elements in modern society, however, that need little encouragement – hedonism, for instance, with its inevitable toll on health and negative role in the welfare of the community at large. My advice would be this: if you wish to pursue the Orphic path, consider carefully the nature of the hero who gave it his name. Then tackle Dionysus, but only after Silenus has accepted you as a pupil – and therein lies the true mystery.

In addition to the aforementioned Mysteries there were many lesser, subsidiary systems of devotion and initiation that probably never made the historical records, not to mention the myriad undesirable elements that masqueraded under mystical-cum-magical banners. Mead refers to the Thaisi, Erani and Orgeones and hints at several other oriental cults that later emerged in Mithraic references. However, the modern student of Greek magic and mysticism is advised against concerning him or herself too much with the suspect historical trivia surrounding some of these cults. Better that he/she discover his/her own personal path to Initiation that is better suited to today's world.

The Eleusinian mysteries continued to provide a source of inspiration to many long after their discontinuance and classical literature abounds with scholarly comments concerning the inspiring and uplifting nature of their rites. As a final tribute to Demeter, one could do no better than quote the words of Mylonas:

'Happy is he who, having seen these rites, goes below the hollow earth; for he knows the end of life and he knows its god-sent beginning.' When we read these and other similar statements written by the great or nearly great of the ancient world, by the dramatists and the thinkers, when we picture the magnificent buildings and monuments constructed at Eleusis by great political figures like Peisistratos, Kimon, Perikles, Hadrian, Marcus Aurelius and others, we cannot help but believe that the Mysteries of Eleusis were not an empty, childish affair devised by shrewd priests to fool the peasant and the ignorant, but a philosophy of life that possessed substance and meaning and imparted a modicum of truth to the yearning human soul. That belief is strengthened when we read in Cicero that Athens has given nothing to the world more excellent or divine than the Eleusinian Mysteries.

Let us recall again that the rites of Eleusis were held for some two thousand years, that for two thousand years civilised humanity was sustained and ennobled by those rites. Then we shall be able to appreciate the meaning and importance of Eleusis and of the cult of Demeter in the pre-Christian era.[9]

[1] D'Alviella, A., *The Mysteries of Eleusis* (Aquarian Press, 1981).
[2] Eliade, M., *From Primitives to Zen* (Collins, 1967).
[3] *Ibid.*
[4] D'Alviella, A., *The Mysteries of Eleusis.*
[5] D'Alviella, A., *The Mysteries of Eleusis.*
[6] Mylonas, G. E., *Eleusis and the Eleusinian Mysteries* (Routledge & Kegan Paul, 1961).
[7] *Ibid.*
[8] *Ibid.*
[9] *Ibid.*

7·ASCLEPIUS AND
EPIDAURUS

Coronis, daughter of Phlegyas, King of Lapiths, had yielded to Apollo and conceived a son. Shortly before she was due to give birth, however, she married Ischys, the Arcadian. A crow that Apollo had left with Coronis to watch over her came at once to inform the god of the girl's infidelity. Apollo, in his rage, cursed the crow, whose plumage turned black as a result, and put Coronis and Ischys to death. Another version tells how these deeds were carried out on Apollo's behalf by his sister, Artemis. The two bodies were placed in the funeral pyre and the body of Coronis was already half consumed when Apollo arrived, just in time to rescue the infant she had been carrying from the engulfing flames and bear him to Mount Pelion, where he was passed to the care of the centaur Chiron. The child became Asclepius, god of medicine.

Chiron taught Asclepius all there was to know about the art of healing and, as a result, the young man began to effect miraculous cures, the news of which spread to mortals and immortals alike. He even succeeded in restoring the dead to life with the help of the Gorgon's blood that Athene had given to him and with a plant, the healing properties of which a serpent had told him. Hades felt cheated of his prey by the exhibition of such skills and complained bitterly to Zeus who agreed with him that mortals must follow their destiny. Thus, Asclepius was seen as guilty of thwarting the order of

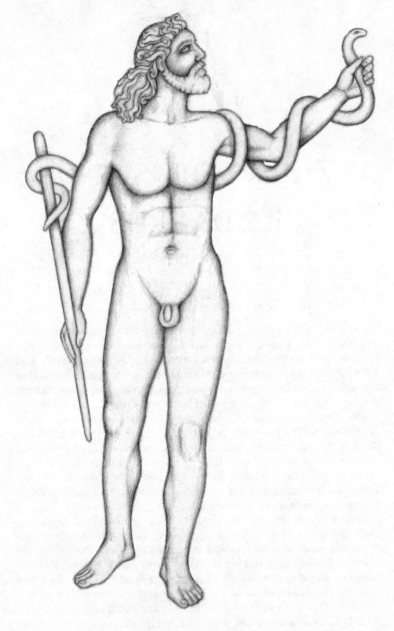

Asclepius with Serpent

nature and Zeus struck him dead with a thunderbolt. Apollo avenged the death of his son by exterminating the Cyclopes who had forged the thunderbolt and for this massacre he was banished from Olympus for a considerable period of time.

At Epidaurus, however, there was another tradition of the birth of Asclepius. Coronis bore her son while her father, Phlegyas, was on an expedition to the Peleponnese, and exposed her child on Mount Titthion where a goat fed it and a dog guarded it. One day, Aresthanas, a shepherd, discovered the baby and was about to take it to his home when he was struck by the supernatural light that appeared around it. Realising the infant was divinely connected, he was careful not to touch it but hastened to report his find to the appropriate authorities. The god of healing was always seen as the offspring of fire or light.

Asclepius was surrounded by subsidiary divinities. There was his wife, Epione, who bore him the two Asclepiads, Podaleirius and Machaon, both of whom were as skilled in medicine as their father. Machaon, in particular, was renowned for his ministrations, having cured both Philoctetes and Menelaus. Machaon was killed at Troy and Nestor brought his body back to Greece. Podaleirius survived the expedition and, on his return, was cast by a tempest onto the shores of Caria where he settled.

Asclepius also had daughters: Iaso, Panacea, Aegle and, above all, Hygieia, who was closely associated with the cult of her father as goddess of health. The final member of the Asclepiun retinue was Telesphorus, the guardian spirit of convalescence, who was represented wearing a hooded cape – the costume officially worn by those recovering from an illness.

THE AESCULAPIUMS AND THE MIRACULOUS CURES THAT TOOK PLACE THERE

Asclepius was sometimes represented as a serpent, but more frequently as a man of middle age with a benign expression. His cult was both a religion and system of therapeutics and his sanctuaries, such as those of Tricca (or Trikki) in Thessaly, Epidaurus, Cos and Pergamus, were always built on specially chosen sites outside of towns, the priests of Asclepius being well aware of the specific nature of Earth energies.

In the cult's early days its medical knowledge was handed down from father to son, certain families holding a monopoly over it, but outsiders were later admitted as neophytes. Temples to Asclepius were known as Aesculapiums. The Aesculapium at Cos was particularly famous because it was there that the great physician Hippocrates founded his first school of rational medicine. The Aesculapium at Epidaurus experienced a long period of prosperity towards the end of the fifth century BC that extended well into the fourth century BC. In honour of Asclepius, a large and impressive temple was erected in which the statute of the god, overlaid with gold and ivory, was kept. The most splendid buildings within the precinct were also raised to honour the god. Prosperity continued until 86 BC when the sanctuary was desecrated by the Roman general, Sulla. A new era opened in the second century AD when the Roman Senator Antonius provided money to rebuild much of the sanctuary.

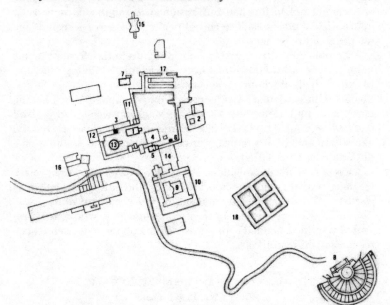

Plan of Epidaurus

1. Temple of Asclepius
2. Temple of Asclepius and of Apollo of the Egyptians
3. Enkoimeterion or Abaton
4. House of the Priests
5. Temple of Artemis
6. Temple of Themis
7. Temple of Aphrodite
8. Theatre
9. Odeon
10. Gymnasium
11. Baths and Library
12. Fountain
13. Tholos
14. Palaestra, Stoa of Kotys
15. Propylaia (Gateway)
16. Palaestra and Hostel for the Athletes
17. Stoa
18. Katagogeion or Guest House

In the Asclepeia special rites were observed. These involved purificatory preparations – baths, fasting, and sacrifices – after which the patient was permitted to spend the night in the Temple of Asclepius where he slept either on the skin of a sacrificed animal or on a couch near the statue of the god. Most famous of all Asclepiun rites, however, were those of incubation, the procedures of which are as valid today as they were in those long-gone times.

The preparation for incubation was calculated to render the patient open to suggestion. This could include various forms of fasting and abstinence, taking part in religious ceremonies at all hours of the day and night, being treated to entertainment of a highly charged content, calculated to induce either extremes of emotional release or alpha-type relaxation. All this led up to the stay in the Holy Hall, by which time the patient had been well and truly conditioned to the fact that he or she would receive a visitation from the god himself or one of his divine assistants.

The visitations of Asclepius were reputed to have taken place during the semi-awake stage usually associated with theta brain patterns, when hypnogogic hallucinations are likely to occur and the mind is most susceptible to auto-suggestion. Genuine dream experiences, however, are said to occur during paradox sleep, when the brain is functioning in delta rhythm and rapid eye movements (REMs) are in evidence. Since accounts appear to vary, the outcome, no doubt, was dependent upon the nature and psychology of the patient.

There has also been much conjecture as to how these visions of divine personalities were achieved, and achieved they were as scarcely a man or woman ever left the holy precincts without reporting at least a cursory glance of the god himself or one of his retinue, and many were able to describe what they had witnessed coherently and with a degree of detail. For example, the vision might advise them to change their lifestyle, take certain medications or avoid the type of thought patterns that inevitably make for ill health. The rationalist will obviously assume that the priests of Asclepius, after dosing their patients with some appropriate hallucinogenic medication, donned the mask of a god or goddess and dispensed their wisdom to the half-conscious patient who, by then, was ready to accept anything he or she might be told.

There has also been much scholarly debate as to which methods the Greeks used to effect this mental submissiveness on the part of their patients. Drugs, perhaps, although hypnosis is the most popular theory. Narcosis is another, although I would have thought that the latter was more likely to induce delta than theta brain waves. Tapes played to people when they are asleep, however, have proved to be effective in some cases, so the priests may well have chanted while the patients slept, although I somehow think not.

The stelae (slabs or pillars with inscriptions and sculptures carved into them) found during excavations that describe the miraculous cures, were doubtless inspired by the priests who would have been quick to appreciate their advertising value. Here are some of the accounts. A man with hideous blotches on his forehead: 'Pandarus, the Thessalian, being asleep, had this vision. It seemed to him that the god covered the blotches with a bandage and instructed him that as soon as he left the dormitory he was to remove it and present it to the sanctuary. At daybreak, as soon as he got up he took off the bandage and, perceiving that his face was now free of blemish, he dedicated it to the sanctuary'.[1]

Another tale involved the child Euphanes who came from Epidaurus: 'Suffering from the stone, he fell asleep. It seemed to him that the god appeared and said to him, "What will you give me if I cure you?" "Ten knuckle bones", replied the child, whereupon the god burst out laughing and promised he should be healed. And in the morning he was'. In another case, a child, deaf and mute from birth suddenly began to speak.[2]

Asclepius was sometimes known as 'the dream sender' on account of his priests' involvement in dream therapy or the interpretation of dreams. Other divinities involved in the Asclepian incubation rites included Hypnos, the winged god of sleep, his son Morpheus, the giver of dreams, and Thanatos, god of death, one of the auxiliaries of Hades who supplied the god with new subjects. Euripides described Thanatos as dressed in a black robe and holding in his hand the fatal sword as he walks among men. Death, however, did not normally appear thus in the myths, being more usually represented as a winged spirit like his brother, Hypnos, who lived with him in the Underworld. Hypnos put men to sleep by touching them with his magic wand or fanning them with his dark wings. He also had power over the gods and Homer relates a story of how, at Hera's request, he took the form of a night bird and sent Zeus to sleep on Mount Ida.

Without doubt, the healing rites of Epidaurus constituted one of the major features in Greek mysticism, as they effected a link between magic and the healing arts that is still observed, albeit in a more modified form, in today's world.

THE MEANING OF THE SERPENT MOTIF

The serpent has always been associated with healing. Hermes' famous staff, the caduceus, consists of two serpents entwining around a central pole, surmounted by a winged orb. The serpents are said to represent the forces of chaos and order that need to be kept in balance if a good state of health is to be maintained. The wings represent the mind's potential ability to control these two opposing factors. In other words, self-healing is the ultimate goal of mankind, but, until we are ready to understand and handle this gift, our health lies in the hands of those who wield the caduceus, who have dedicated their lives to the cause of good health. In the book *Dreambody* (Routledge & Kegan Paul, 1984), by the American psychiatrist, Arnold Mindell, there are several fine illustrations showing Asclepius with the serpent. Mindell tells us:

> The eternal aspect of the snake and its openness to time, life and flow are found in the beneficent feature of Mertseger, the Friend of Silence, who coils up and watches over graves in Egypt. Greece has similar serpents of the dead. Snakes symbolise the vibration of vegetative states, the flow and rhythm of hypometabolic processes that occur during meditation and dreaming and that feel like death (in the positive sense of transcending time).
>
> The two aspects of the snake – its poison and its anti-poison, its time and timeless quality – often appear as two aspects of one archetype.[3]

The archetypal symbology of the serpent really deserves more space than the scope of this book will allow. Jung, Freud and many leading authorities on psychology and occultism who preceded them and followed in their wake, have written copiously on the subject.

The caduceus also establishes Hermes as a Greek healing divinity, while Pan was believed to have rulership over those remedies that emanated from the plant kingdoms. Artemis, Apollo and Athene were the other Olympians concerned with matters therapeutic.

The Greek physicians were well aware of those body energies that have been accorded a variety of names in mysticism, medicine and psychology. Hippocrates (*circa* 460–370 BC) referred to them as the *enormon* and the *physis*, which he believed governed both the body's physical force and sex drive (libido), and its ability to heal itself (the kundalini serpent power ascended to the higher chakras). The medical profession ignored Hippocrates' energy concepts for many years, preferring to focus more on his 'scientific' attitudes and astute observation of cases. In modern times, however, with the growth of alternative therapies, doctors and scientists are at last coming round to the fact that both body and mind are somehow part of an intricate web of energy exchanges, in much the way Hippocrates and the Greek physicians believed. Ancient Greek surgical procedures may have left a lot to be desired, when compared to their modern equivalents, but it was not without good reason that Hippocrates was called the father of modern medicine.

THE INCUBATION RITES

Incubation therapy and its attendant rites were also practised in other Greek cults, notably the oracle of Parsiphae at Thalamai, which was not far from Lacedaemonia. In his *Lives of Agis and Cleomene*, Plutarch describes how one of the ephors (magistrates), had an extraordinary dream after falling asleep at the shrine of Parsiphae. He dreamed that in the room where the ephors met to conduct their business, four of the five seats had been overturned. Shocked by the vision, he heard a voice from the sanctuary announcing that this was in the interest of Sparta. Upon his return to Sparta, the magistrate reported what he had seen and heard to King Cleomenes III. However, the King, who had been secretly planning to get rid of the ephors, suspected him of having invented the dream in order to sound him out. Being eventually convinced of the ephor's sincerity, he took heart and decided to heed the oracle and carry out his original plan. The King therefore gave orders for all of the ephors to be killed and, of the five, only one escaped with his life. These events took place in the year 227 BC.

Here we have the kind of incubation experience that did not appear to involve priests dressing up as gods, although the sceptic would probably argue that someone at the temple was aware of the King's plans anyway, and used the dream sequence as a kindly warning to the visiting ephor. How, then, did he know that one only would be saved? I could go on speculating, but in the final analysis it all depends whether or not you are disposed to go along with the 'god' idea, even assuming the gods to be nothing more than aspects of our own psychological make-up, as many are inclined to believe these days.

In spite of the fact that monotheism dominates western religious thinking, the term 'the gods' often crops up in modern parlance due, I suspect, to the classical emphasis in education. For example, I recently overheard two men in conversation prior to a golf match. One said to the other, 'Well, do you think you can win?', to which his companion replied, 'The gods of golf being willing – yes!' Allusions to 'the will of the gods', 'a gift from the gods', 'the god of music (art, or whatever) certainly passed him (her) over when dispensing his favours' are figures of speech perhaps, but I am inclined to suspect that some unconscious force is at work at a deeper level.

[1] *Flacelière, R., Greek Oracles (Elek Books, 1965).*
[2] *Ibid.*
[3] *Mindell, A., Dreambody (Routledge & Kegan Paul, 1984).*

8·HEROES AND HEROINES

The Greek magical quest is symbolised by the cult of the hero or mortal who, in pursuit of his or her divinity, is subjected to a series of personal initiations that take the form of mythological deeds. These challenges appear in practical, often very earthly forms, in spite of a generous smattering of fabulous beasts, accompanying elemental phenomena and some timely help from Olympus. From an occult or psychological standpoint, these are purely allegorical and simply represent the trials of the aspiring human soul whose quest takes him or her into those universes beyond the dimensions of earthly life and experience, where he or she may eventually be reunited with his or her source. Hercules is the perfect example of the hero, although Perseus, Odysseus, Theseus, Orpheus and many others have been named in the myths.

The Greeks were renowned for their logic. The terms of reference they used to describe the journeys undertaken by those heroic Initiates who ventured from earth to travel the path to Mount Olympus, conquering obstacles in their way and thus gaining right of entry into the company of the gods, were imaginative, highly graphic and psychologically intriguing. The Heroic Path is the way of the individual, albeit with a little assistance from an 'inner planes' tutor and perhaps one or more tutelary deities, it does not refer to the group situation. Many occultists who feel drawn to the Greek tradition may choose to worship in temple form, but ultimately the aspiring hero or heroine stands alone and must face and cope with the oncoming tide of monsters, gremlins and treacherous humans, in addition to his or her own mental weaknesses and spiritual short-comings if he or she is to attain his or her spiritual goal.

A formidable task, perhaps, but in accordance with the Law of Equalities the weapons available to the aspiring hero or heroine are correspondingly powerful. As long as due deference is paid to the tutelary deities (in other words, that the cosmic laws are observed) and appreciation is shown for their bounty, the aspirant will master the ego and receive the well-earned accolades. Should he or she fail, the price or penalty could be heavy: *quem Juppiter vult perdere dementat prius*, or, whom the gods destroy they first drive mad. Of course, it is not really the gods who cause the insanity, but our rejection or misuse of the god-aspects within ourselves that can effect a mental imbalance varying in degree according to the nature and misdirection of those energies. So, while the lone path may appear easier in that you have only yourself to please, the burden of individual responsibility is, correspondingly, a greater one.

SOME COMMENTARIES ON THE HERO THEME IN MYTHOLOGY

Jung sees the hero as closely related to the 'child' archetype, which features strongly in Greek mythology. He commented:

Sometimes the 'child' looks more like a *child god*, sometimes more like a young *hero*. Common to both types is the miracu-lous birth and the adversities of early childhood – abandon-ment and danger through persecution. The god is, by nature, wholly supernatural; the hero's nature is human but raised to the limit of the supernatural – he is 'semi-divine'. While the god, especially in his close affinity with the symbolic animal, personifies the collective unconscious which is not yet inte-grated into a human being, the hero's supernaturalness includes human nature and thus represents a synthesis of the ('divine', i.e., not yet humanised) unconscious and human conscious-ness. Consequently he signifies the potential anticipation of an individuation process which is approaching wholeness.[1]

Abandonment, exposure, danger, etc., are all elaborations of the 'child's' insignificant beginnings and of its mysterious and miraculous birth. The statement describes a certain psychic experience of a creative nature, whose object is the emergence of a new and yet unknown content. In the psychology of the individual there is always, at such moments, an agonising situation of conflict from which there seems to be no way out – at least for the conscious mind, since, as far as this is concerned, *tertium non datur*.[2]

The term 'hero' has, however, come to mean many things to many people, so some distinctions are called for at this juncture. The Spanish psychologist J. E. Cirlot has this to say regarding the heroic archetype:

The cult of the hero has been found necessary not only because of the exigencies of war, but because of the virtues inherent in heroism – virtues which have surely been apparent to Man from prehistoric times and which he has felt the need to exalt, emphasise and record. The magic, the apparatus and the splendour of the very appurtenances of the ancient warrior proclaim the truth of this, as does the custom of according an acclamation worthy of kings to the conquering hero. The relationship between the 'little holy war', that is the struggle with the material enemies outside, and the 'Great Holy War', or combat with the spiritual enemies inside the personality, inevitably gave rise to the same relationship being drawn between the hero of the 'little war' and the champion of the 'Great Holy War'. Every heroic characteristic finds its analogy among the virtues necessary to vanquish chaos and overcome the temptations offered by the forces of darkness. This explains why, in many myths, the sun was identified with the hero *par excellence*. Hence, Alexander the Great is pictured on coins with the horns of Jupiter Ammon, that is, he is identified with the awakening sun of Spring under the sign of Aries. And this leads Jung to state that the most widely accepted of all the symbols of the libido – and he could equally well have said 'the spirit' – is the human figure as the hero – the subject of so many myths, legends and traditional tales. He adds that in the life destined for the hero, the historical and the symbolic are one and the same thing. The first object of the hero is to conquer himself; and this is the reason why the heroes of Germanic legends are usually portrayed with the eyes of a snake. The mythic hero, Cecrops, is half-man and half-serpent. A hero turned Christian is a hero turned knight, with the aid of the saintly warriors such as St George and St Michael.[3]

Regarding those mythical monsters so frequently encountered by the heroes of all pantheons and cults Cirlot comments:

> They are symbolic of the cosmic forces at a stage one step removed from chaos – from the 'non-formal potentialities'. On the psychological plane, they allude to the base powers which constitute the deepest strata of spiritual geology, seething as in a volcano until they erupt in the shape of some monstrous apparition or activity. Diel suggests that they symbolise an unbalanced psychic function: the effective whipping up of desire, paroxysms of the indulged imagination or improper intentions. They are then, *par excellence*, the antithesis – or the adversary – of the 'hero' and of 'weapons'. For weapons are the positive powers granted to man by the deity and this is the explanation of the mysterious, miraculous or magical context of weapons wielded by heroes in myth and legend.[4]

Franz Cumont appears to confirm much of this but also introduces the priestly theme:

> Among those heroes whose merits had opened to them the gates of heaven, – '*virtus recludens immeritis mori caelum*', as Horace puts it, – the military monarchies of the East placed in the forefront the warriors who had died sword in hand in defence of their country, or rather their king. . . .
>
> But, side by side with these valiant soldiers, pious priests were also judged to merit immortality, or rather they adjudged it to themselves. Who could be more worthy to mount to the stars than those who, while yet on earth, lived in their society and in contemplation of them? Then, when Oriental mysteries spread, they all professed to prolong the existence of the initiated beyond the hour of death appointed by Destiny and to exempt them from the fatal law imposed on mankind. Participation in the occult ceremonies of worship becomes an infallible means of securing salvation. The gods welcomed amongst them the faithful who had served them fervently and had purified themselves by the scrupulous performance of rites.[5]

Here the distinction between the martial hero and the pursuant of the spiritual heroic path is clearly drawn, although there is nothing to prevent the warrior from aspiring to the spiritual path. In fact, spiritual warrior rites were practised in many earlier cultures, some of which were nothing if not physically and psychologically demanding.

THE HEROIC PATH AND WOMEN

In order to understand why the Greeks inevitably cast the strong man in the heroic role, one must try to understand the period of history in which these events took place. Patrism had swept down from the north, obliterating the matriarchal system – on the surface, anyway. The rule of force had taken over and countries therefore relied upon their armies to protect the ordinary people, merchants, philosophers, artisans and others who formed an integral part of that culture. If we take a deeper look into the Greek Mysteries we will observe that the sages and seers were just as venerated as the military heroes and, although there was a period in early Greek times when it was fashionable to expose female babies, the goddess cult held a very strong sway, even in Olympian times, priestesses being accorded the same status as priests.

Looking back to earlier times, from 3,000 BC onwards the artefacts that have come down to us from that period certainly seem to indicate that women controlled worship. Crete was later ruled by the Mycenaeans who seemed quite happy to adopt the existing goddess culture. Merlin Stone quotes the following texts from E. Butterworth's *Some Traces from the Pre-Olympian World*:

> Matrilineality, though not universal in the Greek and Aegean world, was widely spread ... the effect of the system of succession to the kingship and to the inheritance of property on the life of the times was immense. The majority of the clans were matrilineal by custom, and the greatest revolution in the history of early Greece was that by which the custom was changed from matrilineal to patrilineal succession and the loyalty to the clan destroyed. ...
>
> The attack upon the matrilineal clans destroyed the power of the clan world itself and with it, its religion ... the history of the times is penetrated through and through with the clash of patrilineal and matrilineal as the old religious dynasties were broken, swept away and re-established ... The matrilineal world was brought to an end by a number of murderous assaults upon the heart of that world, the Potnia Mater [The Great Goddess] herself.[6]

According to both Euripides and Plutarch, young Spartan women

Cretan Snake Goddess

were not to be found at home but in the gymnasia, where they tossed off their restricting clothing and wrestled naked with their male contemporaries. This was the classical age of Sparta, when the veneration of Artemis thrived and women were free and independent. They also had total sexual freedom and, although monogamy was the accepted rule it was not, apparently, taken too seriously.

The serpent motif, so beloved of the Cretan priestesses, was carried over in the heroic figure of Athene. Many scholars opine that the Lady of the Serpents of Crete was derived from pre-dynastic Egypt, or probably Atlantis, the symbology of the serpent having been understood as deeply sacred since the earliest days of recorded history. Athene's serpent or serpents inevitably made their appearance in her statues. A special building known as the Erechtheum stood in the Acropolis alongside Athene's own temple, the Parthenon. This Erechtheum was believed to be the home of Athene's snake which, as we have already discussed, did not owe its origins to the Greek classical period.

Delphi is believed to be the original home of the serpent goddess of Crete, or Gaia according to the myths. Even after Apollo appropriated the site the sacred Priestesses were known as Pythia (Pythonesses), while coiled round the tripod upon which she sat was the snake known as Python. Later the myth tells us that Apollo killed Python, indicating that the old goddess cult had finally succumbed to the shafts of the god of light, or patriarchal principle, in much the same way as Zeus had appropriated the goddess' oracle at Dodona.

Thus, in spite of the overt predominance of males on the heroic scene, there were also many women who were able to pursue their initiations either by way of the priestly class, as with the Pythia and the many priestesses of the Olympian goddesses whose temples were to be found throughout the land, or through some more Spartan or Amazonian-type activity.

When writing on the subject of Greek mysticism on previous occasions I have drawn the reader's attention to certain aspects of the natures of the Olympian archetypes. For example, of the 12 personalities there are six males and six females, and is it by pure chance that they exhibit the following psychological characteristics?

From this we may see that the anima/animus emphasis can be expressed via the masculine or feminine modes. In other words, earthly experiences in either sex affords us the opportunity of many variations on the two main themes. Note how the animus-motivated goddesses are inevitably virgins, inferring the predominance of reason over emotions, while the other three are emotionally-orientated mothers. Among the gods, the artistic Apollo, detached Hermes and

Goddesses		Gods	
Aphrodite	Anima Extrovert	Zeus	Animus Extrovert
Hera	Anima Introvert	Ares	Animus Extrovert
Demeter	Anima Introvert	Hephaestus	Animus Introvert
Athene	Animus Extrovert	Apollo	Anima Extrovert
Artemis	Animus Introvert	Hermes	Anima Extrovert
Hestia	Animus Introvert	Poseidon	Anima Introvert

deeply emotional Poseidon emphasise the anima, while the overtly macho Zeus and Ares join with Hephaestus the craftsman/artisan to represent the emphasised animus.

Another point to be taken into consideration is that the male heroes were frequently assisted by goddesses, which suggests to me that they were being spiritually instructed to balance the animus against the femininity of the goddess. Nor was it always the warrior or virgin goddesses who aided the heroes in their quests, the gentler divinities also having their favourites. Prior to setting out on their much-sung quests, it was often to the seers or oracles that they turned for guidance.

Those women who feel they would like to pursue the Greek Heroic Path may feel more comfortable under the tutelary guidance of Artemis, Athene or Hestia, but, before making a final choice, they should search their own souls and if they are timid, shy or too lacking in confidence to speak up for themselves, they might fare better under the wing of Zeus or Hephaestus. If, on the other hand, they feel reasonably confident in their choice of path, the Mother of the Gods could always show them how to use that confidence wisely, Aphrodite could help them to use it lovingly or Hestia could show them how to use it caringly. Exactly the same applies to those men who would seek the Heroic Path. If you are already the strong, macho type, be like Ares and seek the gentleness of Aphrodite or the continuity of Hestia, while the more kindly or artistic man could learn much from the strategy of Athene.

INITIATION IN CLASSICAL LITERATURE

Let us see what words of advice and illumination on the subject of initiation into the Greek magical path there are to be gained from classical and other scholarly sources. Eliade writes:

> At Eleusis, as in the Orphic-Dionysiac ceremonies, as in the Graeco-Oriental mysteries of the Hellenistic period, the mystes submits himself to initiation in order to transcend the human condition and to obtain a higher, superhuman mode of being. The initiatory rites reactualise an origin myth, which relates the adventures, death and resurrection of a Divinity. We know very little about these secret rites, yet we know that the most important of them concerned the death and mystical resurrection of the initiand.[7]

> For the history of religion, the particular importance of the Graeco-Oriental mysteries lies in the fact that they illustrate the need for a personal religious experience engaging man's entire existence ... Such a personal religious experience could not flourish in the framework of the public cults, whose principal function was to ensure the santification of communal life and the continuance of the State.[8]

Some occultists I know insist that the group ritual experience, as carried out under the auspices of a priest or occultist of superior rank, is essential to initiation. From the aforementioned, it would seem that the Greeks thought not, the *sine qua non* being the inner illumination that was often of such a private nature that it was never recounted to the profane.

Eliade also points out that the history of religion distinguishes three categories of types of initiations: rites of transition from childhood to puberty, secret fraternity rites and mystical vocations. In the Mediterranean and Middle Eastern world of those times the Mysteries were open to both sexes. Although the Graeco-Oriental Mysteries may, at first glance, appear to be accommodated by the second category, on closer scrutiny they may equally be seen to fall under category three.

There would appear to be certain elements in common among all initiatory experiences, no matter which spiritual banner they fly, but, since we are engaged in the Greek theme, let us consider what has been handed down to us on the subject. Eliade quotes the following under the title, *The Epiphany* of the Mystery God:

> Aristides records an experience in which, 'there came from Isis a Light and other unutterable things conducive to salvation.

In the same night appeared Serapis and Asclepius himself, both marvellous in beauty and stature and in certain aspects resembling each other'. All ancient *epiphaneiae* were of the character of a dazzling light. Porphyry knows that, 'the eye of the body cannot bear' the brightness of divine apparitions. The experience of Apuleius, 'I saw the sun shining at midnight', and '*adoravi de proxumo*', refers to such an epiphany. In the Attis cult 'Hail, Bridegroom, Hail, new Light' announced the epiphany. In the *Liturgy of Mithra* we read, 'Thou shalt see a youthful god, lovely in form, with red locks, wearing a white tunic and scarlet mantle, and holding a bright crown'.

By mystic identification Lucius, after the sacrament of initiation, was '. . . arrayed like the sun and set up like an image of the god' before the spectators. The mystes of Attis became himself Attis . . . A Greek papyrus has preserved a magical prayer based on Hermetic theology, in which occur the words: 'Enter thou into my spirit and my thoughts my whole life long, for thou art I and I am thou; thy name I guard as a charm in my heart'. In a similar prayer we read: 'I know thee Hermes, and thou knowest me, I am thou and thou art I'.[9]

Here we have some examples of role playing, which can also be seen psychologically as relating to the stirring of the god-aspect within the higher or transcendental self. Although heroic magic is primarily of the non-role playing variety, there is no reason why the Initiate should not experience these inner stimulations through contact with the chosen deity. As Eliade points out, the pattern peculiar to heroic initiations involves the emphasis falling on victory gained by magical methods, although the Shamanic dismemberment theme does appear in some Greek cults, notably those of Zagreus and Dionysus, which Jung commented upon in some length in his treatise on the Visions of Zosimos.[10]

The heroes of old were inevitably born of a god to a mortal mother, which is in itself an indication that the god force was already sufficiently manifest within them to bring about the essential individuation that is a *must* for every occult Initiate. The abandonment theme to which our attention was drawn by Jung's observations earlier in the chapter appears to occur in many other pantheons, the deserted godling usually being taken in by some poor person from whom he learns the ways of ordinary people plus the skills of manual crafts and the art of self-defence. Greek mythology tends to favour fabulous beings as nurses to these half-divine progeny, but the principle is the same. They are also shown to grow up rather faster than normal, which is simply the myth's way of telling us that their awareness of their quest became apparent to them early in life, probably during those formative years when the majority of us stand perilously poised at the threshold of puberty.

THE BEGINNER'S GUIDE TO THE HEROIC PATH

How then may we, in this day and age, approach the heroic concept or make our first faltering steps along the upward path to our own, personal Olympus? You may, of course, effect a symbolic reconstruction of what you feel the old Eleusinia or the rites of Artemis or Dionysus might have been and enter into these in the group situation or you may join a study group under an instructor who is well versed in Greek symbology. In truth, however, this is not what the Heroic Path is all about. Hercules set out on his Labours *alone* and, although he occasionally received help from Olympus, his tutors or the nature spirits, in the final analysis he alone completed the tasks he had been set and was obliged to produce evidence that he had done so.

Although little has been written on the subject of the Olympian magical system, there are always the classics and the writings of the sages, philosophers and poets, some of which I have already quoted. Care should be taken, however, not to place too much credence on explanations and interpretations provided by historians and experts as the ebbing and flowing of trends in philosophy, psychology, archaeology and religion will have inevitably influenced scholarship over the years. Keep an open mind and see how you feel impressed to interpret the stories. Combine the classics with some of the detail supplied in this book and you will soon form an opinion as to your own chosen path to the Olympian heights.

The two most important steps along the initiatory path will be acquiring a tutelary deity and attracting a tutor. The path of the aspiring hero or heroine being a lonely one, he or she who would venture along it cannot turn to another human for assistance. There is no institutionalised classroom complete with instructor to bail you out of your difficulties and supply you with the answer to the Sphinx's riddles. Every aspiring hero or heroine must place him or herself under the protection of one of the 12 Olympians. Without this tutelage there will be no journey, as there will be no beginning.

The first initiation, therefore, comes in the selection of the correct god or goddess. It may seem odd to some that you need to choose a divine guide in this way, but the aspiring hero or heroine is subconsciously, if not consciously, aware of his or her divine origins and is, therefore, only reaching back to his or her 'parent', be that a god or a goddess. Choosing your tutelary deity is not a decision to be taken lightly – a lot of deep consideration, meditation and study should precede the final decision. It is rather a question of 'Man, know thyself' because in knowing yourself and realising just who and what you are, you will become aware of your spiritual ancestry or cosmic roots.

The god or goddess having been chosen, some form of acceptance will be given. This will occur in a perfectly natural way, perhaps in a dream, in which a location, statue or actual visitation from the deity features prominently or, during the normal course of conversation, someone may unconsciously make a confirmatory suggestion. However, prospective hero or heroine, remember it is between you and your god or goddess, so it will be no use running to a medium for confirmation. If you are unsure, just wait until the all-clear is given from Olympus, as it surely will be.

As for a tutor, that is one thing in the Greek magical system you do not choose for yourself. As the old adage goes, 'When the pupil is ready, the master appears', and this was never more true than in Greek magic. So, if you have not yet been visited by a friendly satyr or centaur, bide your time, your time will come.

In Chapter 5 we discussed how the tutorial role has fallen to these mythical beings, but should this strain your credulity, then the Heroic Path is not for you. There were none more logical than the Greek masters and if the reasoning minds of Plato and Pythagoras experienced no difficulty in grasping these principles and seeing the logic of them, any deficiency we may suffer from in this direction should not be blamed on logic, but rather on our own limited mental conditioning or soul age.

The human brain easily comprehends other dimensions without fear or apprehension *when the soul age is right* and, as long as these altered states of consciousness (ASC's) are ventured into under strict mental control and not via artificial stimulants, then the aspiring hero or heroine has nothing to fear. Should the reverse be the case, however, the phantoms encountered will not be a wise old Chiron, a stern but humorous Silenus or a smiling Pan. Forewarned is forearmed, so enter these realms at your own peril.

First, find your god or goddess who will make you the gift of a magical weapon or instrument. This could be any of those mentioned in Chapter 10 or something designed by the deity exclusively for you. Thus, well-armed, protected and watched over, you may take your first tottering steps. The experience may seem bewildering initially, but then will come the exhilaration as the higher frequencies start to purify your mind and the clear light drops the scales from your eyes.

Of course you will stumble and fall – many times. No tutor or guiding entity would have it otherwise, for how else would you learn? After each wounding and bruising the right healing balm will be handed to you, plus the staff or weapon necessary for negotiating the next encounter that awaits you.

Of course, to the aspiring hero or heroine, Olympus is not just a mountain in Greece where the gods in the image of man sit wreathed in ethereal mists and from which vantage point they lord it over the faithful below, while at the same time participating in the full gamut of mortal virtues and vices. Nor is it a summerland of rest, replenishment and reunion with loved ones where one receives a nice pat on the back for being good. Rather, it represents a state of beingness to which each individual soul from *all* regions of creation may return to be re-absorbed, once it has discovered and developed that god-force within it. We are all gods in the making and we will achieve the Olympian heights *only* when we have overcome our mortality or conquered death through the Path of Initiation. Mortality implies eventual death; the immortals do not die. In other words, they have risen above that state where it is necessary to reincarnate into matter in order to learn and experience. The Greeks no doubt inherited this idea from an earlier and spiritually knowledgeable race, but the concept degenerated as human foibles and weaknesses were superimposed upon the gods to the extent that their original meanings became lost or obscured.

On your way then, dear hero and heroine, and may the gods go with you.

[1] Jung, C. G., Archetypes and the Collective Unconscious (Routledge & Kegan Paul, 1959).

[2] Ibid.

[3] Cirlot, J. E., A Dictionary of Symbols (Routledge & Kegan Paul, 1962).

[4] Ibid.

[5] Cumont, F., Astrology and Religion Among the Greeks and Romans (Dover, New York, 1960).

[6] Stone, M., The Paradise Papers (Virago, 1976).

[7] Eliade, M., Rites and Symbols of Initiation (Harper & Row, New York, 1975).

[8] Ibid.

[9] Eliade, M., From Primitives to Zen (Collins, 1967).

[10] Jung, C. G., Alchemical Studies (Routledge & Kegan Paul, 1983).

9·THE ORACLES

Since earliest times there is evidence to show that man has always been curious about the future. Consequently, anybody claiming foresight has been much in demand. Even in our present age, when reason is believed to prevail, the number of psychic readers is, if anything, on the increase. Many psychologists see this as an unconscious escape from the increasing materialistic emphasis of modern society, but are we really any different from our forefathers and the numerous generations preceding them? I think not. Cicero prefaced his treatise *De Divinatione* with the following words:

> It is an ancient belief, going back to heroic times but since confirmed by the unanimous opinion of the Roman people and of every other nation, that there exists within mankind an undeniable faculty of divination. The Greeks called it *mantike*, that is, the capacity to foresee, to know future events, a sublime and salutary act that raises human nature most nearly to the level of divine power. In this respect, as in many others, we have improved upon the Greeks by giving this faculty a name derived from the word god, *divinatio*, whereas, according to Plato's explanation, the Greek word comes from *furor* (*mania* from which *mantike* is derived). What cannot be gainsaid is that there is no nation, whether the most learned and enlightened or the most grossly barbarous, that does not believe that the future can be revealed and does not recognise in certain people the power of foretelling it.[1]

Some events can, of course, be foretold by science: eclipses, for example, the foreknowledge of which appeared miraculous to our primitive ancestors. These obviously do not contain any specifically psychic content and there is a growing belief, even among occultists, that sooner or later science will crack the time-space barrier so that we will be able to look forward or backward technologically without recourse to the supraphysical.

Although seers are, more often than not, consulted for knowledge of what lies ahead, the oracles of Greece were frequently asked for immediate guidance or advice, as in the case where Oedipus sent Creon to Delphi to find out what could be done to free Thebes from the horror of the plague.

THE DELPHIC ORACLE

The most famous of the Greek oracles was undoubtedly that of Delphi. As we have already established, this was not always sacred to Apollo, having been in existence long before the Olympian imposition. The sun god inherited or appropriated it from previous divinities, notably the Great Goddess of the Minoans, or, Gaia (Earth) herself. This rather suggests that there was some kind of power centre at that location where the 'veil' was thin, rendering it easier for the seer to make contact with other universes or time zones.

The site of Delphi lies at Phocis, in the centre of Greece, some 2,000 feet above the waters of the Gulf of Corinth. Leaving all mystical considerations aside, the sheer beauty of the place must have spoken to the hearts of the men and women who paid fealty to its lords.

Apollo's oracle was presided over by a priestess called the Pythia, who always took care to acknowledge all *genius loci* and former deities whose servants might previously have occupied the prophetic chair – the takeover, according to Aeschylus, having been a peaceful one, and by consent. Included in her prayers were Gaia, Themis, Phoebe, Pallas Pronaia, the Nymphs of the Coricean cave (situated on the Parnassus plateau above Delphi), Dionysus, Poseidon and finally Zeus, father of Apollo. Euripides hastened to correct the statement that the takeover had been one of mutual agreement, however, and spoke of a violent struggle between Apollo and Gaia, the first mistress of the oracle, which was settled by Zeus in favour of his son (*Iphigeneia in Tauris*). The *Homeric Hymn to Pythian Apollo* tends to corroborate Euripides' version. What the poets are probably describing to us is the incoming tide of patrism that appropriated previous matrist strongholds by force.

As we have already seen, the Delphic oracle was by no means limited to fortune-telling. According to Euripides, Earth (Gaia) '. . . conjured up dreams and nocturnal visions that laid bare the past, the present and the future to countless mortals as they slept'. Earth's gift of dream interpretation does, however, give us a clue to the knowledge and nature of the people who might conceivably have known more about the intuitive nature of man than their more logically minded Greek successors.

In those earlier times there was a resident sibyl at Delphi who, we are told, frequently entered the trance state and employed the gift of tongues, which has a Shamanic ring about it. Likewise, her Apollonine successor, the Pythia, was, it is reported, often out of her body when her famous prophetic utterances were made. Even Cassandra, the archetypal seer, was said to become greatly perturbed during certain altered states of consciousness, which rather suggests that prophetic ecstasy was very much favoured in those times, possibly because it was deemed to be more impressive than less dramatic time-probing techniques. The following lines from Diodorus Siculus throw further light on the subject:

> In ancient times it was the goats who first discovered the oracle, which is why in our day the people of Delphi still prefer a goat when they offer sacrifice before a consultation. The discovery is said to have come about in the following manner. At the spot where the *adyton** of the present temple is, there was once a chasm in the ground where, before Delphi was yet a city, the goats used to graze. Whenever one of them approached this chasm and looked down into it, she would begin leaping about in an amazing fashion and bleating in quite a different voice to her normal one. And when the shepherd, marvelling at this prodigious behaviour, examined the chasm to find out what caused it, he himself was affected in the same way as the goats, who in truth behaved for all the world like people possessed, and began to prophesy the future. Later, news of what happened to those who visited the chasm began to spread among the peasants and they flocked to the spot in large numbers, anxious to put the miracle to the test; and whenever one of them drew near, he fell into a trance. Thus it was that the place itself came to be regarded as miraculous, and they believed that the oracle came to them from Gê, the Earth

* The most holy room of the temple to which entry was only allowed to certain people or under specified conditions.

goddess. For a time, those who came hither to seek advice used to proclaim oracles to one another. But, later on, when many people in their ecstasy had hurled themselves into the chasm and disappeared, it seemed good to those who lived in those parts that, for the protection of others, one woman should be appointed as the sole prophetess, who alone should pronounce the oracles. They therefore constructed a device so that she could sit in safety when the spirit entered her and utter her oracles to those who sought advice from her. This device was supported by three legs, hence its name, tripod: and indeed the bronze tripods that we have today resemble it almost exactly.[2]

This rather suggests that fumes or vapour (*pneuma*) of some kind originally emanated from the earth at this point that induced either a state of ecstasy or frenzy or of semi-consciousness which allowed easy access to the subconscious or to any external intelligence with a

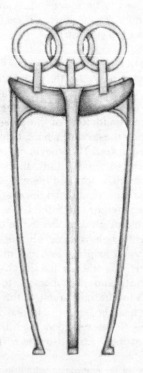

Sacred Tripod of Delphi

message to give. In later times, however, the priests of Apollo staunchly denied this, claiming that the Pythia was not influenced by any external aids, but only by the god himself.

As I mentioned in a previous chapter, Apollo was not always at the beck and call of everyone at his famous shrine, as he regularly took a holiday during the winter. In earlier times, the Pythia only pronounced formal oracles from the *adytum* once a year on the anniversary of Apollo's birth, the seventh day of the month of Bysios, the beginning of spring. Later, she adjusted her schedule to every seventh day (the Sun god's day) of the summer months. During Apollo's absence from Delphi, Dionysus took over, but, according to records, both cults existed happily side by side. Plutarch, himself a priest of Apollo, remarked that, '. . . as regards the Delphic oracle, the part played by Dionysus was no less than Apollo's'. Apollo, being essentially a solar deity, obviously represented the spring and summer months while Dionysus, who took over during the winter months, added a chthonic (underworld) quality to his time at the oracle.

It was possible to obtain a private reading from the oracle for a fee, known as the *pelanos*. These fees could take any form, from sacrifices to the gods to private pay-offs.

Originally, the Pythia was a young girl or virgin, after the style of Apollo's sister, Artemis, but, following an incident when an enquirer took advantage of her and carried her off, it was decreed that the prophetess should from then on be a lady of 50 or more. Writing of the Pythia in the first century AD, Plutarch said:

> The woman who at present occupies the position belongs to one of the soundest and most respected families to be found in Delphi and has always led an irreproachable life, although, having been brought up in the home of poor peasants, when she fulfills her prophetic role she does so quite artlessly and without any special knowledge or talent. Like the young wife Xenophon describes in his *oeconomica*, who should know nothing of the world when she enters her husband's house, the Pythia is almost completely ignorant and inexperienced, so that when she approaches the gods she does so with a truly virgin heart.[3]

There is a school of thought which decrees that intellectuals do not make good psychics as they have a tendency to logicise in their intuitive promptings, which can result in a distortion of the message. Yet, there is always the problem of entities who may wish to impart information of a more scientific or erudite nature, but are limited by the vocabulary or lack of scholarship on the part of the medium. Matters do not appear to have changed much over the centuries!

Some of the details relating to the rites undertaken by the Pythia and her assistants prior to receiving an enquirer are pretty gruesome, to say the least. According to some reports, those who occupied the Pythian tripod in the early days frequently became ill or even died following exposure to the vapours. In later times, however, it seems that the priests of Apollo managed to organise things a little better: the preparatory ritual consisted of a purificatory visit to the Castalian spring, after which the Pythia was escorted to the temple by her train of priests, *prophetes* and clients. Passing through the vestibule (*pronaos*) they entered the central building (*cella*) that contained the altar of Poseidon, the iron throne of Pindar, an *omphalos*,* one or two votive tripods and the sacred hearth upon which Pythia burned laurel leaves and sacred meal. Surrounded by her attendants, she would then enter the *sanctum sanctorum*, or, subterranean chamber from which she would give her oracular pronouncements.

Although the delphic site is well known, it seems that archaeologists have failed to locate the original sanctuary. There is considerable conjecture as to who removed all the traces of it and why. Perhaps the pagans were instructed by Apollo to close the doors or encapsulate the energies until such times as the god was ready to resume his dialogues, or maybe it was the Christians. Nor is there any geological evidence for the existence of those trance-inducing fumes, although it is not beyond the realms of possibility that movements in the earth's subsoil could have caused their original source to close up. Although there have been quite a few guesses made as to how the whole Delphic scene was stage-managed, nobody knows for sure and an air of mystery prevails, but the accuracy of its utterances have been sung by poet, philosopher, scholar and historian, which leaves us in no doubt as to its historical existence.

The difference between Cassandra the sibyl, and the classical Pythia deserve comment. Whereas the Pythia's gift only appears to have manifested when she was seated on the sacred tripod in the Delphic locale, Cassandra's seership was always with her no matter where she went. Can we not read into this yet another indication that the power of the mind should not be limited to ritual or environment but allowed to function freely at any place or time?

---

* *Omphalos*, Greek for navel. A sacred white stone believed to be at the centre of the earth. According to some authorities it was ovoid, while other sources describe it as shaped like a pilaster.

THE ORACLE OF ZEUS AT DODONA

Delphi was by no means the only oracle to be held in high esteem in ancient Greece. Zeus' oracle at Dodona also had a claim to fame. The Pelasgians, ancestors of the Greeks, believed that the voice of Zeus could be heard whispering as the wind stirred the oak trees. Zeus' companion at this oracle was an Earth goddess (later identified as Dione) whose priestesses shared responsibility for its functioning with the representatives of the Father of the Gods. The oak was certainly sacred to Zeus and there seems little doubt that one tree in particular was favoured for the purpose.

Bronze bowls were also employed at this site, the sounds they emitted as the wind moved them being interpreted by the attendants. Clients could also inscribe their questions on sheets of lead, which were then handed to the attendant priests or priestesses. One or two of the answers unearthed by archaeologists show how the people of those ancient times were as much concerned with the trivialities of their lives as those who consult psychics today for advice on how to succeed in business, deal with annoying neighbours or find their true calling in life. Divination by lot is also referred to by Cicero as being connected with Dodona and, as the thunderbolt was Zeus' sacred weapon, all forms of atmospheric phenomena (*meteora*) acquired significance.

THE ORACLE OF TROPHONIOS AT LEBEDEA

This oracle in Boeotia, had a flavour all of its own. Trophonios, it seems, was a local nature divinity who failed to find a place among the gods, but was allotted an heroic role. He had a grotto for his oracle with an opening just wide enough for a man to squeeze through. The whole process of entry was, it seems, somewhat daunting as it involved a difficult descent to the *adyton* under conditions guaranteed to instil fear into all but the bravest hearts. When the clients finally emerged, they were usually in pretty bad shape physically and, although they were often quite confused by whatever had taken place, they were sufficiently aware of the advice they had been given to be able to record it on a tablet for the priests in charge, just to make sure that they had remembered it correctly.

THE AMMON ORACLE

In Libya, the oasis of Ammon apparently sported an oracle that was greatly revered by Alexander the Great. It is described by Diodorus Siculus as being '. . . covered with emeralds and other jewels' and its deliveries involved overt religious ceremonies that were designed to stir the emotions and render clients open to suggestion. Music, dance and ritual were used to achieve the necessary ends.

OTHER ORACLES

The oracle of Parsiphae we have already mentioned in Chapter 6, and there were many smaller and less significant oracles dotted all over the Greek empire. Many of these were Apollonine in nature, while others maintained the strict order of resident sybils that had been passed down since the time of the matriarchal system.

There were also many other famous seers who functioned outside the oracular sanctuaries: Cassandra, Calchas, Amphiaraos, Tiresias and Megistias spring to mind. The messages given by these seers and oracles were seldom initially explicit. Clients were often sent away mystified, the truth only dawning on them when some major occurrence in their life clarified the messages for them. Overall, however, it seems that people were happy with what they received.

OTHER METHODS OF DIVINATION

The Greeks employed many systems of divination in addition to the recognised oracles. The behaviour of birds, fish, animals and natural phenomena were carefully observed and translated into prophetic terms. Many of these methods and signs are as valid to many people today as they were in those distant times. So-called 'old wives tales' differ little from the superstitions of the past, many of which are now being re-examined in the light of new knowledge encountered by the extending frontiers of science and psychology.

In *The Life of Alexander*, Plutarch relates how the great conqueror decided to consult the Delphic oracle concerning his expedition against the Persians. However, he arrived there on one of those days when the Pythia was forbidden to function. Being unaccustomed to observing the rules of others, Alexander sought out the priestess and tried to drag her to her cave by force, whereupon, in exasperation, she exclaimed, 'You are invincible, my son!' On hearing these words, Alexander felt that there was no longer any need for a consultation, Apollo having made his feelings quite clear in that single statement. This belief in *cledones* was clearly related to the belief that words, whether lucky or unlucky, exert an influence, as *cledonismantia* can be defined as the good or evil presage of certain words uttered without premeditation when people come together. Cicero says that the Pythagoreans were very attentive to these presages, and according to Pausanius, it was a favourite method of divination at Smyrna where the oracles of Apollo were thus interpreted.

Some oracles would answer only if consulted in 'cledonistic' terms. For example, certain statues – notably that of the oracle of Hermes Agoraios – were approached by the client who would cover his ears when whispering his request into the ear of the god. He would then uncover them and the first thing he heard would be taken as the god's answer to his question.

The words of children were also heeded by the oracles, the belief being that they are less likely to monitor their statements than adults. In his first epigram, Callimachus describes the visit made by a client to Pittacos of Mytilene, one of the seven sages of Greece,* to seek advice regarding the choice of a wife. Would it be better for him to marry a girl of his own class or seek a wealthier and nobler union? The sage did little more than point to some children playing with their tops in the street and remark 'See them? They will teach you what you should do'. As he approached the group of children, the man heard one of them call out, 'Keep in line', which he immediately understood to mean that he should abandon any ideas he had about marrying for money or rank.[4] Flacelière comments that the famous *Tolle, Lege* of St Augustine's *Confessions*, was uttered by a child and was a cledonistic oracle of the same kind.

[1] *Flacelière, R., Greek Oracles (Elek Books, 1965).*

[2] *Ibid.*

[3] *Ibid.*

[4] *Ibid.*

* The other six sages are Thales of Miletus, Solon of Athens, Cleobulus, Chilon, Periander and Bias.

10·SACRED SYMBOLS AND SUPERSTITIONS

Symbols were of great importance to the ancient Greeks, the most significant being those associated with the various gods, demi-gods, heroes and *genius loci*.

THE BOW AND ARROW

Representing the anima and animus, or, the outgoing and receptive aspects of the personality, the bow and arrow symbolise aiming for a target, seeking out new fields of endeavour or hunting for the 'self'. The tension necessary for the shooting of an arrow suggests the testing grounds of experience: when we are stretched to our very limits, we achieve the furthest distance both spiritually and materially. These symbols are shared jointly by Apollo and his sister Artemis.

THE SPEAR

As distinct from the sword, this symbol has deeper connotations, although like the bow and arrow it is also to be found among the symbols of other early religions and cults, notably Christianity.

In Greek mythology, Athene was able to fell Ares with one blow of her magical spear. Athene is the wisdom archetype while Ares represents brute strength, and yet both were warriors. War is simply an exchange of destructive energies during which both sides stand to lose. Sometimes the vanquished gains more than the victor, so there must be a point in this consideration when logic takes over. Athene did not like fighting for its own sake, but simply engaged in it to help someone or assist a just cause. Her real preference was for her more domestic activities of weaving and embroidery.

Wisdom, the myth is telling us, sometimes needs to meet force at its own level in order to gain the freedom necessary to pursue the path to more peaceful ways. By its very nature it will eventually triumph, for, as evolution progresses, the lower energy frequencies and their accompanying paraphernalia of life must be left behind.

Another interesting point is that Athene, the supreme warrior, was a goddess, inferring that it will be women who will eventually triumph over male-dominated aggression, after which they will be free to return to their domestic preferences in the safe knowledge that war is a thing of the past. Jung believed that the Aquarian Age would be the age of the ascendancy of women during which intuition, caring and the finer qualities of the anima would become manifest at the expense of macho brutality. Athene's spear, therefore, represents those emotional waters of feeling and intuition that can, if correctly understood, overcome brute force.

THE CORNUCOPIA

Fashioned from the horn of Goat Amaltheia, the 'horn of plenty' contained an inexhaustible supply of whatever food or drink was required. It is a reminder that when we give a service to the gods they repay us in more ways than we could possibly conceive. Giving and receiving constitutes an exchange of energies, a barter that is essential for the continuance of the universe in accordance with the Law of Abundance.

EARS OF CORN

We have already noted the symbolism of the sacred ears of corn, which could sprout magically under the direct gaze of the Initiate during the Eleusinian *epopteai*.

Sacred to Demeter, they symbolise fertility and fecundity. Demeter's energies, although they may appear to bear certain similarities to those of Pan, are actually of a different texture, the Pan 'ray' being stimulative rather than reproductive. It should also be borne in mind that the term 'fertility' is by no means limited to the human reproductive processes, but applies to multiplication generally.

THE AEGIS

Another attribute that originated with Amaltheia, the aegis was fashioned from her hide (or some say from the skin of the giant Pallas) to make a breastplate that no arrow could pierce. It is shown as a sort of cuirass (piece of armour covering the chest and back), fringed and bordered with snakes, bearing in the centre the head of the Gorgon Medusa – another version of Athene's fabled shield, which reflects the image of the attacker back on himself.

THE NET OF HEPHAESTUS

We have already seen how Hephaestus used his carefully fashioned net to trap his wayward wife and her Martian lover (see page 33), but, from the magical standpoint, the net is a holding symbol. It signifies that there are times in life when it is best to hold one's fire, sleep on it, take one's time working things out or place a problem or situation in obeyance until you receive some inner guidance as to how to cope with it.

THE HAMMER AND TONGS

The tools of the craftsman, these symbols have the same meaning at the cosmic level as they do in everyday life. Tongs can pick up objects that might normally prove 'too hot to handle' and the same applies to the psychological and magical symbology of the Hephaestian archetype. In other words, anything that is felt to be of dubious origin or meaning is best dealt with via the Hephaestian 'ray' and its symbology.

THE FLAMING CIRCLE

Representative of eternity, the spiritual sun and the return to unity from multiplicity, Hestia's flaming circle emphasises the continuing chain of existence and also the sacred ring of protection in which we may place ourselves when the need arises.

THE CADUCEUS

An archaic emblem that has already been discussed on page 24. There are several other interpretations of the symbology of Hermes' wand, in addition to the order versus chaos concept. For example, the caduceus is also believed to signify the integration of the four elements: the wand corresponding to earth, the wings to air and the serpents to fire and water. As far back as 2,600 BC, it was seen by the Mesopotamians as the insignia of the god who cures all ills, this meaning passing into Greek culture and is preserved in our emblems to this day.

According to esoteric Buddhism, the wand of the caduceus corresponds to the axis of the world, while the serpents refer to the kundalini force which, in Tantrist teaching, sleeps coiled up at the base of the spine. The serpents should always cross at four points, however, double or triple crossings being inaccurate.

THE TRIDENT

The attribute of Poseidon, the trident has magical qualities of a 'claiming' nature. Legend has it that when Poseidon wished to reclaim portions of land that had been annexed by Zeus or some other god or goddess, he would strike his trident into the ground, whereupon the inundating waters would once again ensure that it was returned to his domains.

The Christian devil is frequently depicted carrying a trident (or pitchfork in some cases) and this is believed to suggest Satan laying claim to the souls of men.

Psychologically speaking, it could be seen to represent the deep unconscious, which is always symbolised by the watery depths or any of the several three-fold divisions of the human psychology.

THE ZONA, OR, GIRDLE OF APHRODITE

The cord that forms the girdle, like the chain, is symbolic of binding. In Egyptian hieroglyphics the knotted cord signified a man's name, so it is interesting to find the girdle associated with the personification of the feminine principle. As the most puissant symbol in Greek magic, being more powerful than the thunderbolts of Zeus himself, Aphrodite's girdle tells us that love, if used in its purest context, is the most potent force in the universe.

THE LYRE

The attribute of Apollo in his artistic mode, the lyre betokens the true harmony that music can bring. As with the cithara, the number of strings on a lyre can vary from three to twelve, but the correct number for Apollo's instrument is seven, that number being sacred to him.

The occult concept behind the lyre suggests that he or she who arms him or herself with the power of true harmony, may negotiate the regions of Hades without fear, even Cerberus being charmed into submission by it. Psychologically, of course, the consonance referred to is that of individuation or the harmonising of all factors within the self.

THE FLUTE

This most sacred of musical instruments was said to have been invented by Athene herself. In Atlantean times, the purity of its tone was believed to make contact with the personal resonance of the individual, to the extent that the use of Temple flutes was forbidden to all but those initiated into the sacred science of sonics. Few flutes produce that pure a tone, however, although flute music of a certain type is generally believed to stimulate the kundalini serpent.

THE SYRINX

According to myth, Pan pursued the chaste nymph Syrinx from Mount Lycaeum to the river Ladon where she turned herself into a reed to escape his embraces. As he was unable to distinguish her from the other reeds on the river bank, Pan cut several at random and fashioned them into his famous pipe – a syrinx.

Although fundamentally a nature divinity, Pan was also drawn to music and the dance and, on one occasion, he jokingly dared to challenge the god of music himself to a contest. King Midas was the judge and, needless to say, Apollo walked off with the laurels. They henceforth agreed with each other that Apollo could make his music anywhere that might please gods or mortals, but Pan would confine his melodies to his own territories.

The syrinx, therefore, relates to nature energies. You do not need to actually play an instrument to tune in to its symbolic frequencies – meditation on its shape and beauty will also produce the desired effect.

THE WHITE HORSE

Although an emblem of Poseidon, the white horse was by no means limited to Greek magical symbology as it features in the iconography of several other pantheons, notably that of Celtica. It is probably one of those archaic images that dates back to pre-Flood times when the religious bodies of the period were anxiously placating the sea gods as they observed the ever-rising waters.

In the Trismegistic teachings, the white horse is said to symbolise purified passion, which, like the other Poseidonian signs, relates to our conscious efforts to gain some control over the often turgid waters of the deep unconscious.

THE THYRSUS

The Dionysian, ivy-twined, pine-cone-tipped staff has, like Dionysus himself, dual connotations. As we have already discussed, the dividing line between frenzy and ecstasy is less than a hair's breadth, while the necessity for us to be spiritually reborn at sometime or other during the course of our evolutionary journey is emphasised in many traditions, from the primitive rites to Christo-Judaic Scriptures. The thyrsus symbol indicates that the *misuse* of nature leads to the downward path of chaos while its *positive* use re-establishes us once more on the path to spiritual stability.

THE RAINBOW

Ever the symbol of hope, Iris' attribute suggests the rainbow as the ideal symbol for meditation during the 'dark night of the soul', which is the inevitable lot of all Initiates. A representation of the rainbow in any art-form will always serve to remind us that no condition or adversity is destined to last forever, for sooner or later Iris will arrive from Olympus to advise us of the good news.

THE HELMET OF INVISIBILITY

The symbol and the role played by it in the myths speaks for itself. As with the veil of Nephthys in Egyptian magic, it tells us that it is not always advisable to advertise ourselves or the nature of our quest if we wish to avoid being pursued by the Gorgons of life's iniquities or tortured by our own sense of inadequacy when faced with the spectre of their ugliness.

THE SCEPTRE SURMOUNTED BY A CUCKOO

The cuckoo, who lays her eggs in the nests of other birds, symbolises either the arrival of a spirit or intelligence from a different evolutionary stream or the incarnation of a godling or hero. The accommodating foster-bird acts as a nurse to the alien whose own natural parents are unable to attend to such functions at an earthly level, their species having evolved beyond that point. Hercules was a perfect example of this. Born of an Olympian father to a mortal mother, his descent into matter suggests the god-conscious soul that needs to purge itself of its human weaknesses before it can claim its divinity. A normal birth to an earthly mother is therefore essential, for how otherwise could such a soul know, feel and experience as a mortal?

Zeus cuckolded Amphitryon and the sacred egg he deposited in Alcmene's nest quickly outgrew the smaller nestling and eventually developed the plumage necessary for its long flight back to its own kind. The sceptre is Hera's queenly symbol, while the cuckoo is there to remind us that those exalted souls who choose to incarnate amongst us often select very ordinary environments into which to be born. They may well grow to stand head and shoulders above their siblings, which may cause considerable resentment and therefore much suffering in childhood and youth, but destiny will soon remove them from the restrictive environment of the nest and set them on the road to their heroic quest. They are the souls who have individuated from the collective, so there is, therefore, no native nest here on Earth to which they may return for comfort and succour. Being the 'cuckoo in the nest' is being the odd one out, a syndrome that many of us suffer from in an age where the emphasis is slowly shifting from the material to the transcendental.

THE THUNDERBOLT

This symbol is suggestive of energies of a dissolving and reforming nature. Those false edifices that we have erected around ourselves need to be, like the Lightning Tower of the Tarot, struck down so that we may rebuild them in a more honest way appropriate to the essential expansion of our cosmic awareness.

THE KEY

Hecate's symbol suggests that the key to many of our problems lies in the subconscious, while her hound is Egypt's Anubis or Merlin's Black Dog – that hidden aspect of our psychological economy that can lead us through the dark labyrinths of the mind – the Hades of the Initiate – to the sanity of the sunlight at the end of the tunnel of doubt and insecurity.

THE POMEGRANATE

Regarding the pomegranate, Cirlot says:

... the predominating significance of the pomegranate, arising from its shape and internal structure rather than its colour, is the reconciliation of the multiple and diverse within apparent unity. Hence, in the Bible, for example, it appears as a symbol of the Oneness of the universe. It is also symbolic of fecundity.[1]

This would seem to suggest that those who are experiencing life as a series of highs and lows, uncomfortable though this may be at the time, are at the threshold of a state of spiritual unity wherein they will be able to merge two very important aspects of their fragments to form a cohesive spiritual whole.

This symbol, which is very important in the field of feminine experience, was sacred to both Hera, the frustrated wife, and Persephone, daughter of Demeter, who was obliged to spend a third of her life with her husband, Hades, and the remaining two-thirds with her divine mother in Olympus.

There is something highly sacrificial about this symbology: the fact that Persephone's period spent with her husband was of a 'dark' or unhappy nature, for example, while Hera's constant battle over Zeus' infidelities appears to highlight the kind of suffering that is unique to the feminine experience.

THE PHRYGIAN CAP

According to Spence, the classic cap that the God Mithras is always

Phrygian Cap

depicted wearing, the Phrygian cap, and the mitre have one common ancestry. The cap was traditionally worn by priests offering sacrifices. The male version was surmounted by a crest, comb or point set jutting forward, but, when it was worn by a female, the ornamentation was reversed so that the prominent point fell at the nape of the neck, as with the helmets of the Amazons and Athene's attribute. Cirlot sees it as a part-phallic symbol while its red colour implies renunciation of the self or some other sacrificial significance.

Paris, the Trojan, who was inevitably at the mercy of Eros, is depicted wearing a Phrygian cap, as was Ganymede, cup-bearer to Zeus.

There are many versions of this headgear that have been handed down to our present age. Certain military or ceremonial headgear, priestly garments and simple fisherman's bonnets all follow this style.

THE SIGNIFICANCE OF NUMBERS

Let us examine a few of the superstitions that were observed in ancient Greek times. According to Budge, the numbers to which the Greeks accorded special significance were three, nine and twelve. Cumont has more to say on this subject, however, emphasising the use of mathematics in magical formulae:

> Like the divisions of Time, numbers were divine for a similar reason. The ancients said that they had been revealed to mankind by the motions of the stars. In fact, the progress of mathematics must often have been the result of the progress of astronomy and the former participated in the sacred character of the latter. Certain numerals were thus considered, for astronomical reasons, as endowed with an especial potency: seven and nine, which are the fourth and the third part of the month, seven again and twelve, because they correspond to the planets and to the signs of the zodiac, 360, because that was the – approximate – number of days in the year. To these figures was attributed a peculiar efficacy; thus it was necessary in magical incantations to repeat the operative formula for a given number of times in order that it might produce the desired effect.[2]

The name Pythagoras is synonymous with numbers, Pythagoreans believing that numbers were independent units that possessed certain indivisible and eternal spatial dimensions. The Greeks were well aware, however, that the diagonals of squares are not measurable in whole units, which is why Pythagoras referred to these as 'measureless'. Following on Pythagorean number lore, Nigel Pennick tells us:

Plato (428—347 BC) in his *Timaeus* asserted that the cosmic harmony was contained in certain numbers formed in the cubes and squares of the double and triple proportion commencing at unity. These are created by the two geometrical progressions one, two, four, eight and one, three, nine, twenty-seven. Traditionally represented by the Greek letter lambda, λ, they pervade the European geometric tradition from Greece to the modern era. To Plato, the harmony of the universe was expressed in seven numbers (seven is itself a mystical number): one, two, three, four, eight, nine, twenty-seven, figures which are believed to encompass the mysteries of the microcosm and macrocosm, numbers suited above all others for incorporation in sacred architecture.[3]

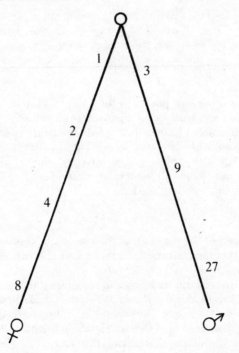

The lambda

The Greek approach to the mystical meanings of numbers has been re-echoed in several numerological systems down the ages and was most pronounced in neo-Platonic teachings. The Victorian scholar, G. R. S. Mead, has covered the relationship between Orphism and allied Greek mystical cults and Neo-Platonism in some detail in his book *Fragments of a Faith Forgotten* (Watkins, 1931) (since this book is somewhat of a collector's item, those interested are advised to order it through the public library system as copies are available in certain major branches).

AMULETS

Healing amulets were often carved from bloodstones (haematite) and frequently featured a serpent or serpents the symbology of which, as we have already discussed, featured strongly in Greek healing. There is also evidence to suggest that the Greeks, in common with many of the surrounding cultures, used wax figures in their magical rites.

THE SWAN

The dedication of the swan to Apollo, god of music, arose out of the mythic belief that it would sing sweetly at the point of death. Although the red swan was the symbol of the sun, it was the white swan which was the most significant, being sacred to Aphrodite. According to Cirlot:

... the swan always points to the complete satisfaction of a desire, the swan-song being a particular allusion to the desire which brings about its own death. This ambivalent significance of the swan was also well known to the alchemists, who compared it with 'philosophical Mercury', the mystic Centre and the union of opposites, an interpretation entirely in accord with its archetypal implications.[4]

THE GREEKS AND ASTROLOGY

It could be said of the Greeks that they were students of astronomy rather than astrology, although in those days the two studies were synonymous.

Astrology, in the form we know and recognise it today, seeped into Greece via Chaldea and Babylonia. When the Greeks first learned of the five planets, they gave them names according to their character. Venus was called 'Herald of Dawn', 'Herald of Light', or 'Vespertine'; Mercury, the 'Twinkling Star'; Mars, the 'Fiery Star' because of its red colour; Jupiter the 'Luminous Star'; Saturn the 'Brilliant Star' or the 'Indicator'. After the fourth century BC, the planets were known by the names of Hermes, Aphrodite, Ares, Zeus and Cronus – probably because the Babylonians dedicated them to Nebo, Ashtar, Nergal, Marduk and Ninib respectively (the gods in one system equating with their counterparts in the other).

One of the earliest recorded Greek astrologers was Thales (639–546 BC). He was reputed to have studied in Egypt, but left no written evidence of his teachings or philosophies. He is famed for having predicted an eclipse that caused much alarm and ended the battle between the Medes and Lydians, the date of which was fixed by the seventh Astronomer Royal in 1835 as being 28 May, 585 BC.

Pythagoras, Anaxagoras, Plato and Eudoxes all studied astrology in Egypt, while Hippocrates used it extensively in medical diagnosis. The philosophers tended to vary in their views concerning the motion of the Earth in relation to the Sun, Moon and planets. Aristotle, for example, believed that the Earth was fixed in the centre of the universe.

Margaret Hone, who was Principal of the Faculty of Astrological Studies from 1954 to 1969, assures us that it was Hipparchus (190–120 BC) who was regarded as the founder of observational astronomy:

> He measured the obliquity of the ecliptic. Making use of Chaldean eclipses, he was able to evaluate the Moon's mean motion. In 134 BC he discovered a new star. He then set to work to catalogue all stars to know if any other new ones appeared. In so doing and comparing with earlier lists, he found that all stars had changed their places with reference to that point in the Heavens where the ecliptic is 90 degrees from the poles of the Earth, i.e., the equinox. He found this could only be explained by the motion of the equinox in the direction of the apparent diurnal motion of the stars. This was the discovery of the *precession of the equinoxes* and was necessary for the progress of accurate astronomical observation.[5]

Here we have a splendid example of the application of Greek logic to an ancient occult art.

Posidonius of Apamea, a Syrian, was also learned in astrology and founded a school in Rhodes that was visited by Pompey and Cicero. His teachings were said to have inspired the *Astronomica* of Manilius. Claudius Ptolemy (AD 100–178) wrote the *Almagest* and the *Tetrabiblos*, both of which exerted a profound influence upon later schools of astrological thought.

Having examined the historical evidence for the rise of astrology in ancient Greece, is it possible to relate the beliefs of these early scholars to the modern study and application of the art? For example, did the Olympian pantheon correspond with the planets or zodiacal signs? The only clue we have is contained in the work of Gaius Manilius (48 BC – AD 20) who wrote:

> Pallas rules the woolly Ram and Venus guards the Bull,
> Apollo has the handsome Twins and Mercury the Crab.
> Jove, with the Mother of the Gods, himself is Leo's lord.
> The Virgin with her ear of corn to Ceres falls, the Scales
> To Vulcan's smith, while to Mars the war-like Scorpion cleaves.
> The Hunter's human part Diana rules, but what's of horse
> Is ruled by Vesta with the straitened stars of Capricorn.
> Aquarius is Juno's sign as opposite to Jove,
> And Neptune owns the pair of Fish that in the heavens move.[6]

At first glance these allocations would seem to have little in common with modern zodiacal rulerships, but perhaps a closer look might prove more rewarding. Athene as ruler of Aries for example, which leaves the broody Ares to cope with the hidden passions of Scorpio. There are many other clues hidden within these lines, albeit psychological ones, for the student to unravel in his or her own time.

1 Cirlot, J. E., A Dictionary of Symbols (Routledge & Kegan Paul, 1962).
2 Cumont, F., Astrology and Religion Among the Greeks and Romans (Dover, New York, 1960).
3 Pennick, N., Sacred Geometry (Turnstone Press, 1980).
4 Cirlot, J. E., A Dictionary of Symbols.
5 Hone, M., The Modern Textbook of Astrology (Fowler, 1975).
6 Hope, M., Practical Greek Magic (Aquarian Press, 1985).

11·DEATH,
REINCARNATION AND
ESCHATOLOGY

The Greeks of old were no strangers to the idea of reincarnation, and their ideas on death are well recorded in classical texts and literature. They were, however, inclined to view the whole process in a broader and more alchemical way, as may be evidenced in the writings of Zosimos of Panopolis, a Gnostic who lived in the third century AD, whom Eliade regards as being one of the most important alchemists of the Hellenistic period. Nor is he the only one to regard the writings of Zosimos as constituting an important part in the structure and understanding of the alchemical principle as it applies to modern psychology. In his masterly work, *Alchemical Studies* (Routledge & Kegan Paul, 1983) Jung devotes a lengthy section to analysing Zosimos' famous visions.[1]

Eliade's approach is an anthropological one, however, but both call for examination if we are to begin to understand the deeper philosophy behind the Greek comprehension of the transmutatory nature of death and rebirth. He writes:

Alchemy deserves special mention. It is important not only because it has preserved and transmitted the Hermetic doc-

113

trines of late antiquity, but also for the role that it played in the history of western culture. Now it is significant that in the work of the alchemists (opus alchymicum) we find the ancient pattern of initiatory torture, death, and resurrection; but this time it is applied on an entirely different plane of experience – that of experimentation with mineral substance. To transmute it, the alchemists treat matter as the Gods – and, consequently, the initiands – were treated in the Hellenistic mysteries: the mineral substances suffer, die and are reborn to another mode of being, that is, are transmuted.[2]

Zosimos' visions involved horrendous tortures and dismemberment, which were shown to him as being an essential sacrificial act of purification before entry into the spiritual realms could be attained. This dismemberment theme runs throughout all initiatory rites, from the Shamanic to the most sophisticated of classical ceremonies in which it was acted out symbolically. Osiris was cut into 14 pieces and reassembled, after which he ascended to heaven, or some ancient Egyptian equivalent to those exalted states we associate with godliness, light and eternal bliss.

What Zosimos was surely trying to tell us is that, unless we purify ourselves of those imbalances that form part of our experience on this planet, by coming to understand them for what they are – no more and no less – we will not ascend to the realms of spiritual sublimity. The initiatory process by which this takes place involves the making and breaking of many bodies, each of which is, has been or will be inhabited by a soul fragment. With the eventual dismemberment (death) of these bodies – or incarnations if you prefer – the soul fragments eventually reunite as a spiritual whole, after which the ascension to those mystical 'higher realms' may take place.

This Mystery teaching obviously originated from an earlier metaphysically knowledgeable race, whose existence has been hinted at throughout this book. What happened later was that those who came in the wake of these original teachers failed to understand that these tortuous refinements were spiritual ones and not necessarily concerned with the mutilation of the physical body as such. It was not until the advent of the philosophers and other civilising influences that symbolism took over from realism in the sacrificial and initiatory acts. The hell-fire and brimstone concept of suffering is, strangely enough, still upheld in certain fundamentalist branches of Christianity. Jung draws our attention to certain parallels between the Zosimos experience and descriptions rendered in the Akhmin manuscript of the Apocalypse of Elijah:

In the vision it is said of the leaden homunculus [little man] that 'his eyes filled with blood' as a result of the torture. The Apocalypse of Elijah says of those who are cast 'into eternal punishment': 'their eyes are mixed with blood'; and of the saints who were persecuted by the Anti-Messiah: 'he will draw off their skins from their heads'.[3]

MENO AND SOCRATES – A DIALOGUE ON REINCARNATION RECORDED BY PLATO

Plato's views of reincarnation are generally known – he believed in it! On the immortality of the soul, he has recorded for us the following short dialogue between Meno and Socrates:

Meno   What was it, and who were they?
Socrates   Those who tell it are priests and priestesses of the sort who make it their business to be able to account for the functions which they perform. Pindar speaks of it too, and many another of the poets who are divinely inspired. What they say is this – see whether you think they are speaking the truth. They say that the soul of man is immortal. At one time it comes to an end – that which is called death – and at another is born again, but is never finally exterminated. On these grounds a man must live all his days as righteously as possible. For those from whom

'Persephone receives requital for ancient doom,
In the ninth year she restores again
Their souls to the sun above.
From whom rise noble kings
And the swift in strength and greatest in wisdom,
And for the rest of time
They are called heroes and sanctified by men'.
Thus the soul, since it is immortal and has been born many times, and has seen all things both here and in the other world, has learned everything that is.[4]

EMPEDOCLES ON THE TRANSMIGRATION OF SOULS

The following fragment from the writings of Empedocles on the transmigration of souls is reminiscent of the Celtic *Song of Amergin* and Taliesin's famous proclamation to Arthur, both of which contain similar descriptions of reincarnatory experiences, adding still more credence to the single source theory:

> There is an oracle of Necessity, ancient decree of the gods, eternal and sealed with broad oaths: whenever one of those demi-gods, whose lot is long-lasting life, has sinfully defiled his dear limbs with bloodshed, or following strife has sworn a false oath, thrice ten thousand seasons does he wander far from the blessed, being born throughout that time in all forms of all manner of mortal things and changing one baleful path of life for another. The might of the air pursues him into the sea, the sea spews him forth onto the dry land, the earth casts him into the rays of the burning sun, and the sun into the eddies of the air. One takes him from the other, but all alike abhor him. Of these I too am now one, a fugitive from the gods and a wanderer, who put my trust in raving strife.
>
> I have wept and wailed when I saw the unfamiliar place.
>
> For already have I once been a boy and a girl, a fish and a bird and a dumb sea fish.[5]

One cannot fail to observe the similarities between the experiences described and those enumerated in *The Book of the Dun Cow*, which deals with the Irish Celtic (Goidelic) mythological cycle.[6]

Greek Concepts of Death, Resurrection and the Afterlife

Cumont tells us that eschatology (from the Greek *eskhatos* – last extreme), that study which is concerned with the ultimate or last things, such as the eventual end of the world, death, judgement and the afterlife, although featured in earlier Greek beliefs, lost credence after philosophical criticism had shown the absurdity of those gloomy tales about the River Styx, Charon's barque and the bizarre punishments that were supposedly handed out to the wicked after death. Whether this applied to the ordinary people, however, I would not care to say, since there are those in our present day and age who still conceive of some medieval hell into which the unjust (usually those who do not adhere to their particular brand of faith) are committed for eternal torture. Cumont backs his statement with Epicurus' teaching that the soul is composed of atoms and is dissolved with the body, while Lucretius praises the Master for having driven from men's minds '. . . this dread of Acheron which troubles the life of man to its inmost depths'.

Adherents to the other great philosophical school, Stoicism, appeared to vary in their views of an afterlife. Ptolemy, for example, was influenced by the Peripatetics, while Vettius Valens chose to accept Stoicism in its purest form. To them, the divine spark or soul became merged after death into the cosmic fires from which it had originally issued, without preserving its individuality. Death was, therefore, a means of liberation from Destiny, by whose bonds they were inevitably bound while here on Earth. Posidonius, on the other hand, although a Stoic, also imbibed the idealism of Plato, so it was all rather a question of personal choice, there being no real hard and fast rules as far as philosophy was concerned.

The pursuants of the Mysteries, on the other hand, did profess definite views as to the destiny of the soul. Unlike the ever-shifting views of the philosophers, the mystics offered a certainty based on divine revelation, corroborated by countless generations who swore to its truths. The people of the times, despairing of the human condition and all that it entailed understandingly welcomed the idea that there was a divine justice somewhere in the universe that would be brought to bear in the next world, if not this. As time progressed, philosophy eventually joined forces with the ancient Oriental mystical beliefs to give the Empire a new eschatology. Cumont remarks that of all the beliefs that emanated from the Graeco-Oriental mysteries, none was to become more influential than sidereal eschatology.

THE DOCTRINE OF SIDEREAL ESCHATOLOGY

The concepts contained within these eschatological Mysteries are too extensive and diverse for inclusion in anything less than a comprehensive study. However, suffice it to say that the spirits of the dead were believed to inhabit the moon, planets, stars or various other heavenly locations, according to their nature and deeds of their earthly incarnation.

Philosophers as far back as Heraclitus taught that the soul was of the same nature as the soul of the universe. At death the body fell to dust and was reunited with the earth, but the animating essence ascended to and became one with the subtle ether that was the source of all life. The official epitaph of the Athenians who fell at Potidaea in 432 BC intimated that the ether had received the souls of those heroes, just as the earth received their bodies.

Plato saw those souls who had made good use of their lives as returning to inhabit those heavenly bodies from which they had originally emanated to partake of divine bliss. Heroes were tradition-ally believed to have been metamorphosed into constellations – Hercules, Perseus, Andromeda, and the Dioscuri, Castor and Pollux, being fine examples.

Stoicism reconciled with astrology in the belief that, as the stars are the most brilliant manifestation of cosmic fire and the soul of man represented an emanation of this cosmic fire, it was only logical to assume that the two would at some point become reunited. Pliny later applauded the astronomer/astrologer Hipparchus for having proved better than anyone else that man is related to the stars and that our souls are 'part of heaven'. Interestingly enough, I recently attended a session at the London Planetarium, when astronomer Heather Couper concluded her oration with the statement, 'We should remember that we are all children of the stars . . .'

Numerous inscriptions attest to the extent that this belief flour-ished, there being an unlimited choice from which to quote. Here are just a couple of examples:

> In this tomb lies the body of a young maiden, *anthophoros* (flower-bearer) of Ceres, carried off by the merciless Fates. But her soul by the goodwill of the Immortals dwells among the stars and takes its place in the sacred choir of the blest.

> My divine soul shall not descend to the shades; heaven and the stars have borne me away; earth holds my body; and this stone an empty name.[7]

The doctrine of sidereal eschatology had several variants to answer the questions Cumont lists as follows:

- who obtains astral mortality?
- how does the soul ascend to heaven?
- where is the abode of the blest to be found?
- how is the blessedness that is vouchsafed to them conceived?[8]

With regard to the first, the Greeks held a variety of views, ranging from wise men, sages and those who had served their country with valour, to ordinary folk who had lived caring and blameless lives within the context of their own class and occupations.

Answers to the second question gave methods for ascending to the stars that were varied and highly graphic. These included rides on Pegasus, ladders into infinite space, rides in the Chariot of the Sun or on the back of an eagle, through the process of etheric levitation, via the miraculous growth of wings, and any other way the people of the time could conceive of to ascend beyond the confines of Earth into the more exalted starry spheres. Doubtless those selling magical formulae made a fair profit from these beliefs.

As regards the third question, the moon was believed to be the lowest of the seven planetary spheres that separated the more violent and restless elements (chaos) and those subject to fate (karma) from that of the eternal gods where all is order.

Where, then, is the abode of the blest? The exact location of the Elysian Fields was debatable, although it was agreed that they were not situated in the depths of the earth. Some saw them as associated with a location between the moon and the sun, while others placed them in the Milky Way or in some far-flung part of the starry universe.

It was believed by many of the philosophers and mystics of the time that the soul had a seven-fold division that corresponded to the seven spheres or seven creations (levels of consciousness between mankind and the Creative Force). Upon death it therefore sheds each aspect (spiritual body?) as it ascends, although there are certain rules involved in this ascension that entail the discarding of those negative passions, amorous desires, misdirected intellect, war-like ardour, ambitious dreams and slothful tendencies that have dominated its earthly life. Having cleansed itself of all such negative traits, it is then ready to merge with the Creative Force. There are, of course, many more considerations that merit mention under this category, but these are too numerous and complex for inclusion here.

In answer to the fourth question, Plato and those who followed in his footsteps dispensed with any ideas of heavenly bliss entailing earthly debauchery, hedonism and the pursuit of purely physical pleasures and saw it in a more sublime and exalted light. Having risen above and beyond the planet to the regions of the starry firmament, the ascended soul could then view all below it in much the same way that we stand over an ant-hill and watch the antics of its builders. Its keener vision will enable it to both see and fully comprehend the sidereal revolutions and, as we would put it today, learn about the creation and workings of the universe.

This is advanced thinking even by many of today's standards, although it would seem to accord with certain interplanetary channelled teachings and the new pagan esoterica that is fast gaining ground among the younger generation.

So, did Galileo and Copernicus really overthrow the system of Ptolemy and vanquish for all times the belief that the stars were peopled by the souls of the dead? Hardly. What has happened is that the whole concept has been transposed to a more metaphysical level – people reincarnate on other stars in other galaxies, so their souls naturally travel to these places. Rather than diminishing these beliefs, modern research, in its exploration of the ever-expanding frontiers of time and space, has added credence to their possibility, so what the Greek sages felt instinctively or intuitively may, at some date in the not too distant future, be proven logically by the empirical studies of science.

[1] *Jung, C. G., Alchemical Studies (Routledge & Kegan Paul, 1983).*

[2] *Eliade, M., Rites and Symbols of Initiation (Harper & Row, New York, 1975).*

[3] *Jung, C. G., Alchemical Studies.*

[4] *Eliade, M., From Primitives to Zen (Collins, 1967).*

[5] *Ibid.*

[6] *Hope, M., Practical Celtic Magic (Aquarian Press, 1987).*

[7] *Cumont, F., Astrology and Religion Among the Greeks and Romans (Dover, New York, 1960).*

[8] *Ibid.*

12·OUR CLASSICAL GREEK HERITAGE

You do not have to look very far afield to note the influence of neo-classicism on our present-day lives. The tall columns that support or ornament our official buildings, monuments and stately homes had their origins in the architecture of classical Greece. The magical knowledge concealed within the dimensions of classical architecture is summed up in the following passages from Nigel Pennick, who commences with a quote from James Fergusson's *A History of Architecture in All Countries*:

> The system of definite proportion which the Greeks employed in the design of their temples was another cause of the effect they produce even on uneducated minds. It was not with them merely that the height was equal to the width, or the length about twice the breadth; but every part was proportioned to all those parts with which it was related, in some such ratio as one to six, two to seven, three to eight, four to nine, or five to ten, etc. As the scheme advances these numbers become undesirably high. In this case they reverted to some such simple ratio as four to five, five to six, six to seven and so on.
>
> This proportion is nowhere as apparent as in the Parthenon

121

in Athens. This magnificent pagan temple, now ruined, was constructed as a replacement for a smaller temple of Athena which had been destroyed by the Persians in 480 BC. Because it was built on the foundations of an earlier temple, which itself had superseded a Mycenaean Throne Room, the Parthenon was laid out in Mycenaean measure rather than the current Greek foot. The major dimensions were so chosen that they were round figures in both Greek and Mycenaean feet, not a difficult task as the measures are related in the ratio of ten to nine. Such a simple relationship is often encountered in related measures such as the Welsh, English and Saxon feet.

The geometry of the Parthenon was such that it incorporated significant measures. Its dimensions were meticulously recorded by an English architect, Francis Cranmer Penrose who measured the temple with a precision to one-thousandth of an English foot. Penrose determined that the Parthenon was not laid out with straight lines, but instead utilised subtle mathematical curves in its fabric. Thus the Parthenon represents another order of geometry, something quite out of the ordinary. Penrose determined that there are essential similarities between the geometrical structure of the Parthenon and the Great Pyramid. The elevations of the fronts of the Parthenon were determined by the Golden Section and the sides were based upon the factor π. Professor Stecchini has calculated that the slight deviations found in the bases of both the Parthenon and the Great Pyramid were deliberate and not the result of slight miscalculations. In his view, the ϕ to π relationship of end to side in the Parthenon parallels that of the north face of the Pyramid (ϕ) to the west face (π). [1]

Greek architecture, in common with the pyramids having absorbed the strong influence of pre-Flood (Atlantean) magical geometry, it is little wonder that (albeit unconsciously) Prince Charles is anxious to see more stately columns and classical lines in today's Britain. Many believe that the Old Country will rise again – perhaps this prophecy alludes to its rising in the hearts of those reincarnated souls who once knew, loved and enjoyed its splendours, the Prince, perhaps, being one of them!

The classical influence upon education needs no elucidation. Greek is still taught as a language in many public and state schools, while the classics themselves constitute an educational foundation in many establishments of learning. Mathematics and geometry are also indebted to the Greek masters, as may be evidenced in many a textbook. Greek drama is still performed in theatres throughout the world and makes up an essential part of most drama training courses. Its verses, along with the myths themselves, have inspired many of the great classical composers, notably Handel (*Semele*), Mozart (*Idomeneo*) and more recently Sir Arthur Bliss' *Pastoral*.

Philosophy is as alive today as it was in the time of Socrates, although the issues at stake have taken a somewhat different turn. At the World Congress of Philosophy, which took place in Brighton in 1988, the subject under discussion, the 'Present and Future of Humanity', elicited some interesting observations from the philosophers present who hailed from as far afield as Africa, China, Latin America and the Soviet Union. The women's movement was also represented by a Dutch philosopher, Dr Maya Pellikaan-Engel, who focused on the strained relationship between Socrates and his wife, Xanthe!

Although the medical profession still regard Hippocrates as the Father of Medicine, it is undoubtedly psychology that has formed the greater partnership with Greek thinking, seeing in the myths and heroic tales parallels between the adventures and endeavours of the human spirit and the psychological economy of man. Jung wrote extensively on the subject.

THE HERCULES MYTH, HIS 12 LABOURS AND THEIR ANTHROPOLOGICAL, PSYCHOLOGICAL AND METAPHYSICAL MEANINGS

My own studies of the subject have been wide and varied, but it was the Labours of Hercules, with their strong psychological and anthropological connotations, that provided me with some vital clues as to the hidden meaning behind the myths.

Hercules was originally named Heracles (pride of Hera) because he was said to owe his fame to the machinations of the Mother of the Gods. The story goes that Zeus, wishing to have a son strong enough to protect both mortals and immortals, assumed the form of Amphitryon in order to lie with the warrior's wife, Alcmene, whom Zeus knew to be a direct descendant of the hero Perseus. Within a few days Amphitryon himself returned from the wars and also lay with his spouse.

Alcmene conceived two sons from these successive unions, Hercules and Iphicles. Expecting his son to arrive on a given day, Zeus swore a solemn oath before all the Olympians that the descendant of Perseus, who was about to be born, should one day rule Greece.

Upon hearing these words, Hera was consumed with jealousy and sought to foil her husband's plan. Hastening to Thebes she deliberately retarded the birth of Hercules and arranged for the wife of one Sthnelus – also a son of Perseus – to give birth prematurely. Unable to break his word, Zeus was obliged to bestow kingship on the first-born child, who was Eurystheus. Having placed her puppet firmly in authority over Hercules, Hera was able to ensure that the hero's life was made as difficult as possible.

There are many stories told of the strength and courage of young Hercules. How he came to be given the Labours is a long tale, involving a period of madness that Hera had deliberately visited upon him, during which he mistook his own children for enemies and slew them. After the realisation of what he had done dawned on him, he consulted the Delphic oracle at whose suggestion he committed himself to 12 years in the service of Eurystheus.

Hercules seizing Cerberus

As mentioned previously, the number 12 is sacred to Greek magic and is also related to the energies of Earth herself. There are 12 signs of the zodiac (and many believe there to be 12 planets in this solar system), 12 apostles, 12 knights of the Round Table, 12 months in the solar year and so forth. So let us assume that the number of Hercules' Labours is no coincidence and no doubt alludes to certain initiatory rites on the one hand and psychological contingencies on the other.

One of the most popular explanations of the 12 Labours is that each task represents the lessons to be learned from the 12 signs of the zodiac (the four-seasoned year has also received mention as represented in Ezekiel's vision of the bull, eagle, lion and seraph, or, man).

In my book, *Practical Greek Magic* (Aquarian Press, 1985), I have given a detailed analysis of what I feel to be one explanation behind these legends, which I see as containing archaic vestiges, initiatory undertones and psychological realities. Unfortunately, space does not permit me to repeat them in this book, but no doubt those interested will make a point of looking them up.

In conclusion, it can justifiably be said that our debt to the ancient Greeks is incalculable. It applies to their fund of knowledge on all levels – material, psychological and spiritual.

[1] *Pennick, N., Sacred Geometry (Turnstone Press, 1980).*

APPENDIX:
PRAYERS AND RITES

The following hymns and fragments that have come down to us from the classical period are a fair representation of the general approach to the religious beliefs of the times.

THE EARTH, MOTHER OF ALL
(*The Homeric Hymns, Homer*)

I will sing of well-founded Earth, mother of all, eldest of all beings. She feeds all creatures that are in the world, all that go upon the goodly land, and all that are in the paths of the seas, and all that fly: all these are fed of her store. Through you, O queen, men are blessed in their children and blessed in their harvests, and to you it belongs to give means of life to mortal men and to take it away. Happy is the man whom you delight to honour! He has all things abundantly: his fruitful land is laden with corn, his pastures are covered with cattle, and his house is filled with good things. Such men rule orderly in their cities of fair women: great riches and wealth follow them: their sons exalt with ever-fresh delight, and their daughters with flower-laden hands play and skip merrily over the soft flowers of the field. Thus it is with those whom you honour O holy goddess, bountiful spirit. 'Hail, Mother of the gods, wife of starry Heaven; freely bestow upon me for this my song substance that cheers the heart! And now I will remember you and another song also'.[1]

CLEANTHES' HYMN TO ZEUS
(Stobaeus, Eclogae, 1, 1, 12)

Cleanthes of Assos (331–233 BC) was the disciple and successor of Zeno as head of the Stoic school. He was the real founder of Stoic theology.

> Most glorious of immortals, Zeus
> The many named, almighty evermore,
> Nature's great Sovereign, ruling all by law –
> Hail to thee! On thee 'tis meet and right
> That mortals everywhere should call.
> From thee was our begetting; ours alone
> Of all that live and move upon the earth
> The lot to bear God's likeness.
> Thee will I ever chant, thy power praise!
>
> For thee, this whole vast cosmos, wheeling round
> The earth, obeys, and where thou leadest
> It follows, ruled willingly by thee.
> In thy unconquerable hands thou holdest fast,
> Ready prepared, that two-timed flaming blast,
> The ever-living thunderbolt:
> Nature's own stroke brings all things to their end.
> By it thou guidest aright the sense instinct
> Which spreads through all things, mingled even
> With stars in heaven, the great and small –
> Thou who art King supreme for evermore!
>
> Nought upon earth is wrought in thy despite, O God.
> Nor in the ethereal sphere aloft which ever winds
> About its pole, nor in the sea, save only what
> The wicked work, in their strange madness,
> Yet even so, thou knowest to make the crooked straight.
> Prune all excess, give order to the orderless:
> For unto thee the unloved still is lovely –
> And thus in one all things are harmonised,
> The evil with the good, that so one Word
> Should be in all things everlastingly.

One Word – which evermore the wicked flee!
Ill-fated, hungering to possess the good
They have no vision of God's universal law;
Nor will they hear; though if obedient in mind
They might obtain a noble life, true wealth.
Instead they rush unthinking after ill:
Some with a shameless zeal for fame,
Others pursuing gain, disorderly;
Still others folly, or pleasures of the flesh.
(But evils are their lot) and other times
Bring other harvests, all unsought –
For all their great desire, its opposite!

But, Zeus, thou giver of every gift,
Who dwellest within the dark clouds, wielding still
The flashing stroke of lightning, save, we pray,
Thy children from this boundless misery.
Scatter, O Father, the darkness from their souls,
Grant them to find true understanding –
On which relying thou justly rulest all –
While we, thus honoured, in turn will honour thee,
Hymning thy works forever, as is meet
For mortals while no greater right
Belongs even to the gods that evermore
Justly to praise the universal Law![2]

THE INITIATES IN THE ORPHIC-PYTHAGOREAN BROTHERHOOD
ARE TAUGHT THE ROAD TO THE LOWER WORLD
(*The Funerary Gold Plates*)

Thou shalt find to the left of the House of Hades a spring,
And by the side thereof standing a white cypress.
To this spring approach not near.
But thou shalt find another, from the Lake of Memory
Cold water flowing forth, and there are guardians before it.
Say, 'I am a child of Earth and starry Heaven;
But my race is of Heaven (alone). This ye know yourselves.
But I am parched with thirst and I perish. Give me quickly
The cold water flowing forth from the Lake of Memory'.
And of themselves they will give thee to drink of the holy
    spring,

And thereafter among the other heroes thou shalt have
lordship.
(*Plate from Petelia, South Italy, fourth to third century BC*)

I am parched with thirst and I perish – Nay, drink of me
(or, But give me to drink of)
The ever-flowing spring on the right, where the cypress is.
Who are thou? . . .
Whence art thou? – I am the son of Earth and starry Heaven.
(*Plate from Eleuthernai in Crete, second century BC*)

But so soon as the spirit hath left the light of the sun,
Go to the right as far as one should go, being right wary in all
things.
Hail, thou who hast suffered the suffering. This thou hadst
never suffered before.
Thou art become god from man.
A kid thou art fallen into milk.
Hail, hail to thee journeying the right hand road
By holy meadows and groves of Persephone.
(*Plate from Thurii, South Italy, fourth to third century BC*)

Three more tablets from Thurii, of roughly the same date as the
previous one.

I come from the pure, pure Queen of those below,
And Eukles and Eubuleus, and other Gods and Daemons:
For I also avow that I am of your blessed race.
And I have paid the penalty for deeds unrighteous,
Whether it be that Fate laid me low or the gods immortal
Or . . . with star-flung thunderbolt.
I have flown out of the sorrowful, weary circle.
I have passed with swift feet to the diadem desired.
I have sunk beneath the bosom of the Mistress, the Queen of the
Underworld.
And now I come a suppliant to holy Persephoneia,
That of her grace she send men to the seats of the Hallowed.
Happy and blessed one, thou shalt be god instead of mortal.
A kid I have fallen into milk.[3]

The similarity between these texts reinforces the idea that there was
within the Orphic tradition a single funerary rite that only varied
slightly according to location. No doubt people of the future who

might chance upon the occasional copy of the Book of Common Prayer would form the same opinion of ourselves.

RECONSTRUCTION OF INCUBATION RITE FOR MODERN USAGE

As we have already discussed in Chapter 7, page 73, the incubation rites were cleverly organised by the priests to ensure that the participants were sufficiently pre-programmed to receive information from the god, or those acting on his behalf. However, here are a few guidelines for those of you who would like to experience a healing rite of this nature, in simplified form.

Important THE RITE SHOULD BE LED BY SOMEONE WHO IS AN EXPERIENCED PSYCHOLOGIST, PSYCHOTHERAPIST OR HYPNOTIST WHO IS ALSO SKILLED IN INTERPRETING DREAMS, A BELIEVER IN THE EFFICACY OF THE RITE AND/OR THE HEALING POWERS OF THE OLD GODS.

During the three days preceding the performance of the rite, those taking part should keep to a very light diet, avoiding all meat products, alcohol, drugs and stimulants of any kind. There is no actual limit on the number participating in the pre-incubation ceremony, but for obvious practical purposes, as most of us live in comparatively small houses and do not have access to the Aesculapiums of ancient times, the fewer the better as the participants will be obliged to sleep in the same house for the night of the rite. A proper conference centre would probably be the best venue, as long as those officiating are schooled in the building of a psychic atmosphere appropriate to the Greek gods of healing (or erecting a temple on the inner planes).

The participants should make a day and night of the ceremony, meeting early on the morning of the chosen date. Plenty of exercise in the fresh air should be taken, and if there are swimming or sauna facilities available for a ritual cleansing, then so much the better. The body should be thoroughly cleansed both externally and internally.

Although a day's fasting would be preferable, in today's busy and exhausting world, a light diet of fruit, with plenty of natural spring water would do just as well. Those wishing to robe for the occasion should wear as much white as possible and avoid all dark colours. Silver, gold or yellow, amethyst, light blues and nature greens are also acceptable to the Greek deities of healing.

The afternoon should consist of an encounter group or similar in which each member is given the opportunity to discuss his or her ills, with an analysis as to what he or she feels to have caused them. Particular attention should be paid to frustrations, guilt complexes, and the breaking down of past conditioning to make way for the reprogramming energies of the rite. This should be followed by a period of relaxing entertainment, preferably not of a bawdy or lewd nature. A good drama or classical concert can usually be guaranteed to loosen tensions and allow easy access to the subconscious, but ecstatic or frenzy-inducing activities are not advised in the context of this version of the rite, the emphasis being on the transpersonal or higher self.

As most people these days tend to end the day fairly late the final meal should not be eaten too early, although it will only be very light, in keeping with the dietary instructions. An hour or so prior to sleep, the group should meet together under the direction of the Leader for its incubation instructions. These will be delivered during a guided meditation in which the participants will be introduced to Asclepius, and perhaps one or two of the other gods or goddesses of healing, in accordance with the preferences of the group. For example, in a goddess-orientated gathering, Athene, Artemis or Hygieia might be preferred, while a polarity-orientated group might prefer Asclepius and his daughter, or Artemis and Apollo. During this experience the participants should be encouraged to allow the chosen deity(ies) to envelop them, so that they become thoroughly familiar with their frequencies. The Leader should then give the final instructions, which will involve explaining to the group how each of them will receive a visitation from the god or goddess, who will make it known to them why they are experiencing the particular disorder before bestowing the healing touch. Should the condition involve an unpaid karmic debt, the night's dreams will offer some explanation. In fact, the reason for the illness or disorder will be made quite clear in the ensuing dream patterns. If the Leader is trained in hypno-therapy he or she should instruct the group using hypnosis and end with an invocation to Hypnos, God of Sleep, Morpheus his son, the Bringer of Dreams, and the chosen deities. The company should then retire for the night.

For those who are inclined to forget their dreams by the time they wake up, a pen/pencil and notepad should be kept beside the bed so that if they wake up in the night they can quickly jot down their experiences. Nightmares might well occur, as these will be manifestations of the 'shadow', id or unwanted phantasms from the deep unconscious that need to be expunged as they might possibly be the cause of that person's distress. On the other hand, some may experience ecstasy and actually 'feel' the touch of a god or goddess.

Intense dreaming can also produce hypnopompic hallucinations, or, the short-lived persistence of the dream-image on awakening.

The following morning, the group should meet first thing to discuss their night's adventures and exchange experiences, which will then be analysed by the Leader. The outcome should lead to a better understanding of the reason for any disorders or illnesses and, in some cases, there may well be a miraculous healing.

I have deliberately refrained from giving set prayers or meditations for this rite, as I feel that these should be chosen by the Leader according to the nature of the members of the group and the conditions for which they are seeking the aid of the gods of healing. The rite can also be enlarged upon or diminished to accommodate the venue and circumstances, but the essence must be the ritual cleansing of body and mind to prepare for a visitation from a higher frequency.

I have also kept the rite in the Greek mode, as this is a book about the Greek Tradition, but it can equally be transposed into the framework of other systems. After all, in Graeco-Roman times the Iseums (Temples of Isis) throughout the Empire specialised in incubation therapy, especially for those who were suffering from stress or nervous disorders – yes, they had them in those days, too! A similar procedure was employed, except that it was Isis or her daughter, Bast, the Cat Goddess, who appeared to the sick, either in their dreams or during that transition period just prior to sleep when the mind is particularly susceptible to hypnogogic visions.

[1] *Eliade, M., From Primitives to Zen (Collins, 1967).*

[2] *Ibid.*

[3] *Ibid.*

BIBLIOGRAPHY

Budge, E. A. Wallis, *Amulets and Talismans* (Collier Books, New York, 1970).

Cirlot, J. E., *A Dictionary of Symbols* (Routledge & Kegan Paul, 1962).

Cumont, F., *Astrology and Religion Among the Greeks and Romans* (Dover, New York, 1960).

D'Alviella, G., *The Mysteries of Eleusis* (Aquarian Press, 1981).

Eliade, M., *From Primitives to Zen* (Collins, 1967).

    Rites and Symbols of Initiation (Harper & Row, New York, 1975).

Fergusson, J., *A History of Architecture*.

Flacelière, R., *Greek Oracles* (Elek Books, 1965).

Graves, R., *The Greek Myths*, Volumes I and II (Penguin, 1984).

Hone, M. E., *The Modern Textbook of Astrology* (Fowler, 1975).

Hope, M., *Practical Celtic Magic* (Aquarian Press, 1987).

Hope, M., *Practical Greek Magic* (Aquarian Press, 1985).

Hope, M., *The Psychology of Ritual* (Element Books, 1988).

Jung, C. G., *Alchemical Studies* (Routledge & Kegan Paul, 1983).

Jung, C. G., *Archetypes and the Collective Unconscious* (Routledge & Kegan Paul, 1959).

Karpodini-Dimitriadi, E., *The Peloponnese* (Ekdotike Athenon S.A., Athens, 1986).

Kerenyi, C., *The Gods of the Greeks* (Thames & Hudson, 1979).

Larousse Encyclopedia of Mythology (Hamlyn, 1959).

Mead, G. R. S., *Fragments of a Faith Forgotten* (Watkins, 1931).

Mindell, A., *Dreambody* (Routledge & Kegan Paul, 1984).

Mylonas, G. E., *Eleusis and the Eleusinian Mysteries* (Routledge & Kegan Paul, 1961).

Pennick, N., *Sacred Geometry* (Turnstone Press, 1980).

Spence, L., *An Encyclopaedia of Occultism* (Citadel Press, New Jersey, 1960).

Stone, M., *The Paradise Papers* (Virago, 1976).

Witt, R. E., *Isis in the Graeco-Roman World* (Thames & Hudson, 1971).

INDEX

Only major references are given. Page numbers in italics refer to illustrations.